Action Filmmaking Presents:

The Youtube Producer's Handbook

2nd Edition

Action Filmmaking Presents:

The Youtube Producer's Handbook
2nd Edition

By Nathyn Brendan Masters

Interact with TimeCode Mechanics
Website: *www.timecodemechanics.com*
Email: *timecodemechanics@gmail.com*

If you like this book please review it
and tell others about it.

Published By
TimeCode Mechanics
timecodemechanics@gmail.com

©2015-2017 Nathyn Brendan Masters and TimeCode Mechanics

ISBN-13: 978-1979408479
ISBN-10: 1979408475

Printed in the USA.

To
All My Friends, Fans and Supporters

Acknowledgments

Cover Images:

www.pixabay.com
Geralt https://pixabay.com/en/users/geralt-9301/
Kulinetto https://pixabay.com/en/userskulinetto-6689062/

Extra Images:

Kulinetto https://pixabay.com/en/userskulinetto-6689062
Stocksnap https://pixabay.com/en/users/StockSnap-894430/

TABLE of CONTENTS

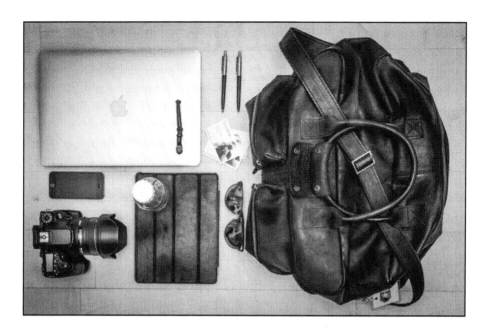

A WORD FROM THE WRITER

Hey guys, Nathyn Brendan Masters here with a new one. Okay, it's not really a new one, but an update to an old one. This is the 2nd edition of the Youtube Producer's Handbook. In the first book I really focused on filmmaking, but in this one I talk more about being a Youtuber in general, so if you have the first one, not much has changed aside from that, and the book itself being more tightly edited.

I wrote this book after writing a similar book called "Action Filmmaking," which detailed writing and producing a no budget, independent action film. With the DSLR craze in full swing, many creators made their own films. It started when photographer Vincent Laforet, considered the father of HDSLR Cinema, got his hands on a Canon 1D and did a short film called "Nocturne," which showed off the camera's incredible progressive shooting and low light abilities. Then he dazzled us with an amazing short called "Reverie" on the Canon 5D Mark2. "Reverie" not only showed off the 5D's lowlight capabilities and color management, but it's ability to get the depth of field indie filmmakers had been trying to get for years with adapters and camera hacks.

These cameras became the new Holy Grail for indie filmmakers. Then came the 7D, T2i, 70D, T3i and a slew of affordable 1080/24p HDSLRs. Canon became the King of the low/no budget indie film camera market.

But now it's all about mirrorless, micro four-thirds, low light, EIS and 4K. Sony and Panasonic (who started the 24p video craze), are now the go to brands, as Canon waited way too long to introduce a 4K camera and JVC (the creators of the HDV format), seem to have been lost in the shuffle.

Cameras get smaller and smaller and even action cameras shoot some version UDH 4K (check out my book upcoming "Action Camera Filmmaking") either natively or via interpolation. Camera tech has improved so much and is so attainable, the barrier to entry is all but gone.

I wrote the first edition of The Youtube Producer's Handbook after my low budget martial arts action film, "Wages of Sin" did so well on the platform. After over 600,000 views, because of some weird Youtube shenanigans, it ended up getting removed. I did eventually re-upload it, and sits at just almost 400,000 views.

Though the film never regained the momentum it had, I realized Youtube was a new way for indie filmmakers to be seen and actually make some money from their work, versus dealing with shady distributors and door keepers. I also did filmmaking tutorials, tech reviews, EDC videos and more while getting paid via ad revenue.

In 2013 I released *Epitaph Bread and Salt*. "Epitaph" was an action horror movie based on my comic book series of the same name. The movie took off almost immediately and has been seen by over a million people. Then I released the action thriller "Crisis Function" and the horror film "The Perfect Letter"a year later, all of which did well. With that, I decided to write a book about filmmaking for Youtube, and it pretty much replaced Action Filmmaking.

But what goes up, must come down. In 2015 Youtube announced it was changing its algorithm. People who were making money mainly from getting into the suggested feed were going to take the hit. This was done to mainly to take down commentary and reaction channels, but it hurt everyone because the "suggested videos" where how most new people were discovered.

Most of us experienced a hard economic decline and the irony is: it didn't work. Commentary and reaction channels are still around, but many creator's earning were cut, some by as much as 70%.

In 2016, angered over financial losses and the US Presidential election, The Wall Street Journal and the mainstream media took aim at Youtube blaming creators for fake news, conspiracy theories and basically everything wrong with the world.

The WSJ ran a hit piece on Youtube superstar PewDiePie, taking some of his jokes out of context and branded him a Nazi supporter. They did similar things with others as well and many times didn't even try to hide the fact they were lying as they new many wouldn't fact check or even read the whole thing, just the headline. But companies still pulled ads from Youtube to the tune of 750 Million dollars causing a major crackdown cutting content creator profits even more. Some were cut completely.

In 2017 advertisers started coming back, ad revenue got better and many more videos continue to be uploaded each day, so now is the time to get in while the getting is good. Your work can still be seen and you can still profit from your work if you know what you're doing. And I'll keep telling people what I know, to help make that happen.

-Nate

CREATING YOUR YOUTUBE CHANNEL

The Coveted Youtube Partnership: What It Actually Means...

Youtube is the most watched "network" in the world. An international, digital, interactive television network. What's placed on Youtube indeed has global significance and can be watched in almost any country that allows open access to the internet. This is what you are becoming part of. You will need a Gmail and Youtube account to start.

The Youtube Partnership basically means you profit from ad revenue on Youtube. You make content and then give Youtube the permission to place ads before and after (and in the middle of, if long enough) the content that you create. With enough videos watched by enough people you can actually make a living wage.

This is not something that will happen overnight in most cases. It can take days weeks, months and sometimes years to get notice unless you're actively uploading everyday or you're uploading content people specifically want to see and know is being uploaded.

To become a Youtube Partner you must be eighteen or older (or have your parents sign you up) and you must enable your account for monetization. To do this your account must be in good standing, which means you haven't violated any of the community guidelines or (and this is the big one) uploaded copyrighted material to your account. Your channel must also have a minimum of 10,000 views.

To get started log in to your account and navigate to your Channel Settings page in the Creator Studio (click on your avatar's drop down menu to get there). Go to "Features" click the "Enable" button by monetization. Once you read and agree to the terms of service you can move on from there.

Go back to your "Channel Settings," click the Monetization tab. Select "How will I be paid?" then click "associate an AdSense account." The Google AdSense site will ask you to associate your Youtube account with a Google account, (if you have Gmail, that's your account). Enter your information and you're on your way to Partnership. As a partner you will get...

• Free, unlimited HD uploads (uploads not limited to fifteen minutes).

• YouTube Analytics (The ability to see demographics and the amount of money being made).

• Audience engagement features: comments, subscribers, social features.

• Custom channel branding.

• Annotations and InVideo Programming.

• Creator Academy. (Free courses on creating for Youtube)

• Creator Playbook with tips and best practices

• Help Center resources

•Advanced product features (custom thumbs, series playlists, Associated Websites & Merch Annotations, Live*)

•Eligible to apply for advanced programs (YouTube Space access and development programs)

•Strategic and technical support

•You can also place ads at the times you want them to play on your ten minutes or longer videos.

Naming Your Business/Channel/Production Company

You should come up with a name for your company. The name should be original and not cliché. Company titles that sound *cool* and involve words like reel, cut, film, etc are cute, but subject to being already taken. Your channel name may also be different from your business.

Do a Google search for the name you do come up with and see if someone is using it or some form of it. One of our special effects guys was using "Windy City Effects" but another person (who started later) used "Windy City F/X" and then sued the original name owner for copyright infringement because the newer company had more clout with the insiders.

Companies can have similar or even the same name provided they aren't doing the same business. Chicago is called "The Windy City" so a Chicago company named "Windy City Effects" is awesome, but also very desirable and predators with more access to legal maneuvering will be tempted to steal it.

To protect your name a good thing to do is to get a credit card in that name and use it to buy business supplies a few times. Once it's used in commerce that will aid in proving when the name was first used legally. Also having a website helps because registrars list when the site was first registered and who (or what company) registered it.

A body of work also helps. Companies with a big body of work that has been copyrighted have a certain amount of protection. If you copyright under the company name the date of copyright will also reveal who obtained the copyright (and would include what company if you list it). Also constant media placement especially online, will help people find you with the click of a mouse. Also keep in mind, when starting, quantity over quality seems to still be an effective way of building a channel.

There is no other company called TimeCode Mechanics. It's an original name (ironically I am mainly a line of sight video editor and the only time I ever look at a timecode is to properly line up sound and special effects) the name does imply that I do something with film or video; namely edit or fix it, which I actually do, but mainly for my own productions. We do take small video or editing gigs from time to time, but those are far and few in between.

This is the kind of company name you want to have. When people Google your totally original name all they will find is information about you. This is actually important as you may gain people seeking to follow you.

Create Your Logo
Once you have your name you need to create a logo, one for print and one for screen. These logos can change every ten years or so but should consist of the same elements. On film, elements can move and shape to form the logo. If you have the money or the know-how you can also create an animation and even special fonts for your company.

Once created this can be trademarked so if anyone uses it without permission, under certain circumstances they can be sued as well as people who create logos too similar to your own. And while the Trademarking process is, many times, long and drawn out, fear not, you can copyright the design too.

You may want to pay an animator if you can't do the animated logo yourself. If you watch big movies, their logos say it all. Some people say they can even tell an indie film from a big film simply by the way the logo comes on the screen.

Licensing Your Business

You may also need to obtain a business license. If your primary business is shooting weddings, that's what you want to get the license for. Unless you're shooting films professionally and making real money, stick with the primary thing you use your camera for. Also be sure to get a PO Box in the name of your business ASAP so you can start correspondence. PO Boxes are generally cheap (at least they are here in Chicago) so don't use your home address. Some places may require a license to get a PO Box, some just require your name on office company stationary, which can be easily made on any computer with a decent word processing program.

Basic Company Structure for a Youtube Partnership

In "Action Filmmaking" I went over the corporate structures you can use to set up a business, but for this, the one you want is Sole Proprietorship. This is controlled by you. There are no partners, all the profits are yours and at any given time funds can be transferred from your business to your personal account and in fact they can be one and the same, but probably shouldn't be. You will need a Federal Tax ID Number - (EIN) and can apply for one online. They're decently quick to get and you can open a bank account under your company name with this.

The biggest drawback to this is a Sole Proprietorship does *not* protect you from lawsuits. And while these suits are probably frivolous, you still have to spend money to file and defend these. What a Sole Proprietorship does do is protect your company name. Your name is legal now and on file with the government, including a date it became "real". The government is your witnesses.

Another aspect of the Sole Proprietorship is you're only responsible to yourself. Profits will indeed be yours, but also losses. The money goes in, but also comes out of your pocket. Everything you do is on you. The majority of businesses in America are indeed Sole Proprietorships.

Don't Lose You Account Or Your Profit

You want to keep your account free of Content ID Matches and definitely free of content strikes. Even royalty free and public domain content has set off Content ID alarms and gotten copyright strikes Create your own content as it's safer. (See "Using Music on Youtube" in the "Editing and Post" section of this book). If you get a viral video, expect someone may try to steal your profits. A lot of scammers are out there so learn how Youtube's copyright system works from top to bottom.

Selling DVDs of Your Videos

Youtube is copyright neutral, meaning they do not own the copyright to your material and you can still sell recordings of your movies if you're doing feature length content. If you're going to be selling DVDs at conventions, festivals or shows, you'll want to get a credit

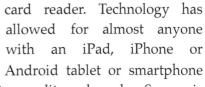

card reader. Technology has allowed for almost anyone with an iPad, iPhone or Android tablet or smartphone to get a credit card reader. Square is probably the most popular, but there's a number of readers out there to choose from.

Register your reader and link it up to your bank account (or Paypal if your reader allows for that) and once you download the software and all that good stuff you're ready to go. The reason behind this is simple; at many shows people may want your product, but may not have actual cash on hand, but may have their ATM or credit card. This will allow you to get the sell, whether they have actual cash on hand or not. And I've seen it come in handy in a number of occasions and even ma and pop businesses are using these readers.

Better Than Old School Distribution?

With the old school indie distribution model you had to wait around for someone to decide if they wanted to buy your film or not. But now the choice is yours and you control what you want people to see and when and how you want to release it. You're in the driver's seat.

Even Better Than Vimeo?

Vimeo also has **Vimeo Pro**, a set up where people can pay to watch your indie films and videos. It cost about $20 a month and you can charge a fee. Vimeo is a big enough company and known all over. The difference is, Youtube has no upfront cost. You join and call it a day. You have to pay Vimeo for what Youtube does for free. Also people would prefer a free movie and don't mind sitting through six-second skippable commercial breaks.

Your Youtube Presence

How you present yourself on Youtube will be how fans and viewers come to know you. The photos and images you chose for your channel header and profile picture need to be exactly how you want people to see you. If you're a tech guru, your images should be tech related. If you do movies you should have images that represent the kinds of movies or shows you make. If you don't know Photoshop you may have to have someone make a backdrop for your channel, but plenty of people will do this for you for cheap, or even free if they like your content. You should be tweeting and pushing images to Instagram as well at least a few times a week.

All of this is key as not only do you want your videos seen, but you want to gain an audience. You are now the product. People will watch your movies, buy your merch and support you if you give them reason to. Just make content people want to see. It's harder than it sounds, but easier than you may think.

Business Plan

Make a business plan. Since we already know the project is going to Youtube, your business plan has to do more with pulling the project together and marketing than distribution. Your plan needs to consist of:

1. Who you already know and what they can bring to the table
2. What equipment you have versus what you need
3. What is the goal of your film? Are you going to festivals, seeking a distributor or self-distributing (see more on this later)
4. Don't forget that special props list
5. What's your next project going to be?
6. How will you pay and get paid for this project?
7. How will you spend or save the money if any is made?

All of these are important things to consider.

CHOOSING YOUR CAMERA AND GEAR

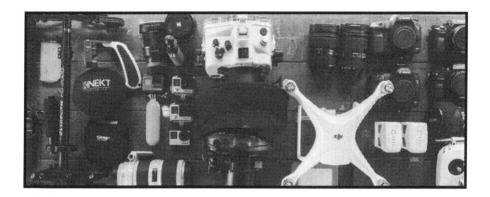

What You Will Need

A modern computer with lots of speed: I'll assume you have a computer or access to one. If you can afford it I suggest a Macbook Pro or iMac running Final Cut Pro X. Doesn't have to be new, but at least able to run FCPX. On the PC side there's many options. I suggest the computer have an up to date processor. I have a 2012 Non - Retina 15 inch Macbook Pro and it rocks (but it also has two graphics cards). You should get the best machine you can afford. On the PC side there's tons of inexpensive laptops and user upgradeable desktops available. The more processing power and speed, the better.

An **HD or UHD (4K) Camcorder or HDSLR:** The old standard was a camera capable of imputing data into a computer by way of "Firewire" or what others called IEEE 1394, the standard invented by Apple Computer that made digital filmmaking really possible, but it's been pretty much fazed out by card and drive based cameras, higher USB rates and Thunderbolt. Todays standard is a camera that records to swappable media or an internal harddrive and is plugged up to the computer via USB, then the footage is moved to a harddrive. The harddrive you work from will probably be an SSD (Solid State Drive) connected via USB 3 or USB C.

A Tripod: You need stabilization for most shots and everyone needs a decent tripod. Tripods start at around $40 and can get up to about $1000 or more. A decent one with a good head can be had for around $200 via eBay.

You want a fluid head to get smooth shots. You also want a tripod that can hold over ten or more pounds if you're going to have a rig or cage.

Stabilizers: Gone are the days of basic tripod shots. In the past the Glidecam, Fig - Rig and similar devices were big, now it's all about gimbals, stabilized lenses and EIS (Electronic Image Stabilization). While Glidecam style stabilizers and other human powered methods are still used, mechanical hand held options like the **Zhiyun Crane** have become more popular, especially with lighter weight cameras. And there's a gimbal for almost everything; from DSLRs to iPhones, someone makes a gimbal for it.

Shotgun Mic: You should have a shotgun microphone and a boom-pole. You can buy an extending mic stand from Radio Shack for about $30 and unscrew it from the base. A good shotgun mic can run you from $150 up. Azden makes some good ones on the cheaper end and again, there's always the $130 shotgun mic plus boom pole kits on eBay. It's a good deal.

The $300 **Rode Video Mic Pro** is probably the most sought after on camera microphone, but the **Rode Video Mic Go** and **Video "Micro"** are also decent low cost options for on camera microphones. Then there's the Zoom line, the H1, Hn, H4n and H5 all which are used to do sync sound just like the old days of film or can jack right into the camera's audio ports. I have an H1n and it's awesome stuff. The sound is solid and you can screw it on to a monopod or light stand and leave it.

For sit down commentary style videos or voice over there's the Blue Snowball and Blue Yeti, both inexpensive high quality microphones that plug directly into your computer's USB port.

Lighting: Today many Youtubers and indie filmmakers alike use inexpensive LED light panels. A super bright Fancier Studio 500 LED light Panel (500 watt equivalent) with dimmer switch can be had for $100. Smaller light panels can be had for less than $40. LED lights are very bright, but consume less energy. Many of them can be operated on both electric and battery power (usually Sony NP-F550/F750/F960 series batteries) making them also a portable option as well.

Old school lighting kits can start out costing about $200 for a three light kit. The bulbs will cost about $10 for a 500 Watt and $5.00 for a 250 watt daylight bulb. These bulbs are usually sold at camera shops. You can also find them on Amazon or eBay. You may even find them cheaper at B&H.

You can also take the cheaper "indie" route, which is go to Home Depot and grab three $30 halogen work lights, the kind with the yellow stands that raise and lower, then set them up. These give off 250 to 500 watts of light. White balance your camera accordingly and you're good.

Editing Software: Once you shoot everything you will need to do post, that's putting it all together. Editing software can go from basic stuff that just puts your footage in sequential order, to high-end stuff that will allow you control over everything from color correction to music. You get editing software for free with Macs and even some Windows computers now, but this is far from professional grade.

Extras: In the past there were extras I suggested you invest in, but today the list of extras are almost a "must have" for a slick look. In the past a "Stickypod" or a jib arm or a steadycam would make your camera movements and shots stand out as more professional, but today it's a whole different story. As technology trickles down and quality gets better, people are creating things to get a professional look. When I first wrote this book I suggested the low budget filmmaker get a few extras, but stray away from a spending a ton of money, but now I'm going to get into the extras, but keep in mind you'll want to have access to eBay and Amazon.com to shop as only an indie filmmaker can.

Now you're probably going to want a shoulder mount and a slider depending on the kind of content you're doing. Shoulder mounts sit on your shoulder and help keep the camera steady. This can take the place of dollies for tracking and moving shots.

Now if you've been researching this you know that shoulder mounts can go all the way up to $400 and sliders can get up to $300. But I'm going to point out some things. When you hear people talk about eBay shoulder mounts or eBay sliders they're talking about various companies that make these things, but are not huge companies. If the quality is good these small companies actually become known because of the low price. But many times these companies don't promote their names, so they are only known by the place people bought the item...eBay. On eBay a simple and effective Kamerar SLD-200 23 slider cost $85, but a Kessler slider cost almost $500 brand new.

A shoulder mount can cost upward of $300 or more, but there's so many other options now it's ridiculous. The Cowboy Studio mount is pretty popular for around $30 and the Spider Steady (those unnamed rigs with the blue handles that look like Transformers) go for $80, and then there's the countless nameless economy mounts. But go to Youtube and search for "Shoulder Mount" or "Shoulder Rig" and you'll see a bunch of these in action.

To check out cameras you should find your local camera rental house and ask to see the image quality. Don't be afraid to play with the settings. Look through the viewfinder and LCD screen and try to get the image you want. A lot of effects are done in the computer while others are done in camera. If you don't have a camera store look at the reviews and forums to see what people are saying.

The Best Camera is the one you have with you....

I personally believe in owning equipment. Even if cameras change, you'll always need lights, tripods, dollies, etc. You should own at least 1 HD camera. If you can't afford a high end camera, at least get one of the older Canon Vixia cameras or a T3i, they're incredible and are amazingly cheap right now. The Canon EOS M3 is about the same price as a T3i and is new and more compact, which is perfect for vlogging. Be sure the camera shoots 1080p at 30fps and most have a 1080/24p mode now for filmmaking.

Gone are the days of DV. Entry level cameras are now HD and tiny pocket sized cameras can do 4K video, so let's take a look at what we have now. The choices are enormous. Considering the idea behind this book, the cameras listed here will still not go over a $2000 price tag and will still start under $200. And as always, there are a lot more cameras out there than the ones I'm listing, but I'm listing the ones I would (or do) shoot with and why.

Also, you'll notice I still include tape-based cameras. Just like I included DV cameras in Action Filmmaking even though HD was the big thing, in this one I'm including tape-based cams because people still use them even though most, if not all, new cameras are storage based, meaning they store footage to a built in disc or storage card of some sort.

I do try to stay up to date as much as possible, but this is video technology. By the time you read this there will be possibly many more new cameras out. Your best bet is to subscribe to a Youtube camera review channel like Kaiman (Kai) Wong, Think Media or Tom Antos, myself (TimeCode Mechanics) and many others to really seek out current info. These cameras go from old to new. The older models can usually be found used on eBay.

Action Cameras

Tiny helmet or vehicle mounted cameras like the **GoPro Hero** (probably the most known brand) are called sports or "Action" cameras, specifically used to strap onto bikes, suction to dashboards or carry on a selfie stick to get a first person perspective, or record the user while in action. They can also be used in films for the same purpose. Because they're small, compact and many times cheap, depending on brand, they're very common today. They typically shoot 1080/30p and 720p at 30fps and 60fps and newer ones can shoot 2.7K and some form of UHD 4K either interpolated or native at 30p and 24p. Most come with a waterproof housing for underwater use.

The original GoPro sales on eBay for about $100 or less including waterproof housing and mounts. The GoPro Hero2 and Hero 3 White and Silver are also about $150. The Hero 3 is said to be sharper and able to produce higher quality stills. The Hero 3 "Black" is also about $150 and has a few extras and the ability to shoot 4k at an awe inspiring "12 frames per second!" (Huh? Why?).

Seriously, the current crop of GoPros shoot 4K video; the coveted GoPro Hero 5 Black shoots true UHD 4K (not to be confused with Cinema 4K) at 24p and is currently running around $400. The Go Pro Hero 6 does 4K at 24p and 60p, has a 2 inch touch screen and works on voice command. It also has advanced stabilization and cost $500.

Don't have GoPro money? Several cheaper lines of Action Cameras are being made, my favorite being the SJCam cameras, probably most know after GoPro. They're cheaper, but still get great quality images. The basic SJ4000 model shoots at 1080p/30p and can be found for about $69 on Amazon or eBay (or even less at Gearbest for the basic 1080p model). **The M20**, a tiny 4K/24p (interpolated) native 2K action camera with built in LCD  screen, great on board audio (for an action camera) and advanced gyro image stabilization makes for a perfect grab and go camera for up and coming vloggers and others who want a small camera that's light and out of the way. This one, as with the others, has a wide angle lens and a 16mp Sony sensor. This camera sells for around $100 or less depending on where you buy it.

The **SJ6 Legend and SJ7 Star** are two of SJCams latest cameras, the SJ7 being a native UHD 4K action camera with an aluminum body, 12mp sensor and great battery life. The camera is capable of a slew of frame rates, but currently lacks 24p (but they're working on it), instead going with 30p and 25p Superview as well as 2.5k at 60fps.

The SJ6 is also a 4K camera, but this one, like the M20, uses interpolation and is actually a 2.7K camera natively with a 16mp sensor. While it lacks the metal body, it has a built in tripod hole, making it one of the few action cameras to be able to be mounted directly to a selfie stick or tripod without the housing. Both cameras have a mini USB microphone jack and low light modes. By the time you read this the SJ8 should be on the way, boasting 4K at 24P (tentatively)/25P and 60p, a 2.5 inch touchscreen, EIS (Electronic image stabilization) up to 4k/30fps and an external GPS.

MgCool is the company behind the Explorer line of action cameras, including the Explorer Pro and Explorer Pro 2 and upcoming Explorer 2c.

These cameras are less expensive and at times can be a little more clunky, but they get the job done.

I reviewed the Explorer Pro, a generally basic, but decent action camera, using a lens technology called "Sharkeye" to get clear images. The Explorer Pro 2 is touch screen while the upcoming Explorer 2c (which should be out by the time you read this or not far from it) is said to have 3 scene modes, a light painting function and also capable of 20mp stills. These are all interpolated 4K cameras. The Explorer Pro and Explorer 2 sell for around $100 and the Explorer 2c sells for about $150.

HDSLRs

The Digital Single-Lens Reflex camera or DSLR has changed the scope of modern day indie filmmaking the way the DVX100 did in 2003.

In the beginning DSLRs where the choice of the modern day professional photographer who wanted to get a great image from their camera and process it quickly, leaving behind the old darkroom chemical process for a digital one.

But things exploded in 2008 when Canon announced the 5D Mark 2. A groundbreaking DSLR (or sometimes called an HDSLR - High Definition Single Lens Reflex camera) that had the ability to shoot full HD. While the Nikon D90 shot 720p video, the 5DM2 shot 1080p and did so with a full frame sensor which allowed greater light and an overall better image.

Then came Vincent Laforet, a photographer who was part of Canon's "Explorers of Light" education program and who also just happened to be a Pulitzer Prize winner. As the story goes he wanted to see what the camera could do and managed to talk someone in the company into allowing him to give one of the prototypes a test run. This resulted in a short film called "Reverie". The film hit the internet and the rest is history. Millions of hits later Vincent Laforet was a household name in the indie filmmaking world and pushed Canon to the forefront of indie filmmaking.

Canon used to be the king of the HDSLR market. I've personally seen a 5D used as B-cam for a RED. If you can't afford a 5D Mark II (which are now running around $1000 on eBay). Currently the camera is on it's fourth incarnation. There's several other cameras being used to get as close to that award winning Canon image including the 7D, 60D, and the very popular T line: The T2i, T3i, T4i and T5i which are loved because of the price to quality ratio. You get footage that looks pretty close to the 5D for much less. The Mark IV runs about $3,000, body only, and has a 30mp sensor and is capable of 4K video using the mjpeg codec.

Because Canon was late to the 4K party, their popularity wavered. Panasonic and Sony and even GoPro started producing 4K capable prosumer models and fans snapped them up. But don't count Canon out yet, their EOS M line has gained some heat with entry level vloggers as well as their G7 X and G7 X Mark 2 with flip up screens and the great video and stills quality Canon is known for, and though expensive for 1080p video, it's a no brainer for many who don't need or care about 4K.

Also in this vein is the **Sony RX100** line of expensive, but highly functional 4K compact cameras used by many vloggers such as Casey Neistat, Roberto Blake and Sara Dietschy. While the price is high you'll get great images and that low light Sony is known for. The flip-up screen makes this camera a hit with the high end vlogging community. These

cameras are generally small and can be dropped into a jacket pocket, which makes it a great, but pricey, grab and go camera. Also it's a fixed lens camera so you won't be swapping out lenses anytime soon, but then again, if you wanted interchangeable lenses, you wouldn't have bought an RX100.

Currently the Panasonic G7, in my opinion, is one of best cameras for Youtube production. A lot of vloggers and content creators use it and it's relatively inexpensive. Little brother of the GH5 and the G85, the G7 is a UHD 4K, Mirrorless Micro Four-Thirds Digital Camera. The camera has a 16 Megapixel live MOS Sensor, Venus Engine 9 Image Processor and 2.36m-Dot OLED Viewfinder.

The reason this camera is so well loved and received is also because of its price to quality ratio. In Youtube production you're always looking for the best quality equipment for the lowest price. Until your channel starts making money you're going to want to pinch every penny. But if you want great quality, but you're on a budget, this camera can be had for around $500, body only. The G85 is around $900 and the GH5 can be taken home for about $2000 and that's body only. All of these do great quality 4K, but the GH5 does professional quality 10 Bit 4:2:2 4K.

Black Magic Cinema Cameras

Like I said, you won't be seeing the RED in this section, but the Blackmagic Design Cinema Camera you will see. On the high end of this list the Blackmagic boast a 2.5K Image Sensor capable of 12-bit RAW, ProRes and DNxHD Formats, 13 Stops of Dynamic Range, 23.98, 24, 25, 29.97, 30p Frame Rates, EF and ZE Lens Mount, LCD Touchscreen with

Metadata Entry, SDI Video Output and Thunderbolt Port, Mic/Line Audio Inputs, records to Removable SSD Drives, and it includes DaVinci Resolve and UltraScope. But what's great about it is it comes in just around $1000 — $1500 (under $1000 in some places), putting it right in the price range for those indie filmmakers with a little more cash. But the downside is, most people would only use this camera if they're going to print to film otherwise shooting RAW does nothing for you, but take up space (and lot, meaning money spent on a large RAID system) and after a while the quality gains would go unnoticed for any other form of output aside from a film print.

This also goes for its 4k big brother which comes in at just under $2000 at B&H Photo which again falls into our price range. But just as with the 2K, what are you going to do with all that RAW 4K footage and where are you going to store it?

While it looks good on paper the indie filmmaker has to consider things like that. If you're working with even a Terabyte harddrive RAW footage for a feature will eat that up, not to mention removable SSD drives are in no way cheap. So you'd be shooting high end indie stuff on a camera like this. Not to mention you will HAVE to do color correction because these cameras shoot flat.

The Black Magic Pocket Cinema Camera uses a use a Super 16 imaging area and is capable of 422 ProRes capture with lossless CinemaDNG added via firmware and it also uses interchangeable lenses. This thing records to 64 gig SDXC cards which is definitely easier on the indie filmmaker's pockets and/or

pocketbook. But definitely there is a wide array of things to work with. Again, this camera also records flat and it's not something you're just going to do point and shoot work with, you have to know what you're doing in post and during shooting.

BlackMagic also offers the Micro, with a Super 16mm-Sized Image Sensor, Active Micro Four-Thirds Lens Mount, 13 Stops of Dynamic Range, that Records Full HD 1920x1080 CinemaDNG RAW, Apple ProRes 422 (HQ) at 220 Mbps. Its compact design allows it to be attached to higher powered drones and be used as a drop or crash cam. The camera has an expansion port with radio control ports, an SDHC/SDXC Memory Card Slot and HDMI & Composite Output, 3.5mm audio in. This is a $1000 camera, that shoots at 1080p. While the footage is high quality, I'm not sure who the audience is for this camera at that price point. Also the monitor is sold separately, as there is no on board video monitoring.

While you may be thinking these cameras are overkill for Youtube, there are many people doing great work with all of these cameras on and better on Youtube right now.

iPhones and iOS Devices

The iPhone

As we know if you need something done, the iPhone probably has an app for that, including filmmaking. (We'll get to that later). The iPhone 8 has an "advanced 12MP camera". The sensor is said to be larger and faster with "deeper" pixels. But it has optical image stabilization which is preferred over EIS. While most don't usually seek out the iPhone just for Youtube videos, some have decided to see just what can be done with these little cameras. Obviously there's no real focusing system, F-stops or any of that stuff (that will be remedied later, so keep reading), but with the right amount of light it captures a great 4K image and is obviously lightweight. There's even steady cam attachments for it. Honestly, people have been using their phones to vlog forever at this point so nothing really new here.

iPad/iPad Mini

Like the iPhone there's no real control over focusing, F-stops etc, but with good lighting the image can rock! But what's awesome about the iPad the amount of attachments made for it. While there's a ton of attachments for the iPhone, the iPad mini has its own set of indie filmmaking and video production add-ons to help turn the iPad into a video or still shooting dynamo.

The Makayama Movie Mount for the iPad/iPad Mini is one such add-on. It not only allows for you to attach the iPad to a tripod, but allows you to attach 37mm conversion lenses, so while you may not have control over your image you can control your field of view. But guess what, that's not all...

Magnetic Lenses: There's several companies that produce magnetic lenses for use with phones. Simply affix a magnetic ring round the camera's built in lens and then you're able to place the new magnetic lens to fit right over the camera's lens allowing a wide angle, macro or telephoto lens to be added. This kind of adapter is also non destructive and also allows your iPhone/iPad to continue to fit into all those cases you bought for them over time. But seriously, these little attachments let you know that people are paying attention to the indie market! And remember how I said you had no control shooting on the iPhone or iPad? Well...

FiLMiC Pro is an app that actually allows you control over your focus and iris separately, there's zoom control, settings for slow and super slo-mo and even has a choice of frame rates allowing you to record at either 24p, 25p (pal) and 60p. But the thing that blew people out of the water was you can control your MBPS (megabits per second) and can get up to an insane 100mbps which is actually more than the Canon 5d Mark 2. You will need more space too.

Drones:

This is a new section for the book, drones. There's so many of them, so I'm just going to hit on the main ones and one of the more inexpensive ones. Since the 2015 - 16 era and the rise of vloggers like Casey Neistat, drone footage has become a big part of Youtube's landscape. They're even reviewers who specialize in drone reviews.

While drone shots are completely unnecessary for the average a Youtuber, some well placed drone footage makes a video more enjoyable, "likable" and "shareable" (makes the user want to like and share it). Poor use of drone shots makes a video look overdone and tired, but a good use of drone shots will pull a viewer deeper into the video's locations and story.

If you can afford one, the **DJI Phantom** drones are the favorite of many Youtubers today. While the Phantom 4 and Phantom 4 Pro can be purchased for around $1,000 the Phantom 3 Standard is a steal for around $500. Around the holidays you can catch these drones on sale  at places like B&H photo or on Amazon.

The Standard is probably the one you want as a beginner as it has quite a variety of functions that will help the n o v i c e drone pilot quickly get into the swing of t h i n g s ,

while still being powerful and enabling the user to get great land and cityscapes from a sweeping bird's eye view.

If you have an even bigger wallet and want to impress all your friends and passersby, then you want the $3000 DJI Inspire 2 paired with the $2000 DJI Zenmuse X5S Gimbal camera then you can shoot 12 bit RAW footage from a drone camera. Shooting RAW is shooting footage that preserves most of the image information without processing or compressing it. (Not to be confused with the term "raw footage" simply meaning unedited footage). The large files take up a lot of space and processing power to work with.

For $1000 you can get the **Mavic Pro,** also loved because of its size. It can be folded up and placed in a backpack, carryall or messenger bag. Its clocked at 65 KMPH, or roughly 40 MPH , with 27 minutes of flight time and a 12mp camera on a 3 axis gimbal.

But if you're not made of money, there's plenty of low priced drones you can buy, that will support cameras or have cameras already built in.

The Bugs 3, is a drone from MJX that gets rebranded all the time. I o w n personally the D r o c o n version that cost around $150 or less depending where you get it, Amazon tends to have the best deal on these. While it doesn't have all the bells and whistles the DJI has, it does get the job done.

It has brushless motors, gets 15 to 20 minutes of flight time and can be controlled from 300 - 500 meters away. It also has two way communication between the unit and the remote which lessens lag time making the Bugs 3 very responsive, especially for a drone in this price range.

Unlike the pro drones, the Bugs 3 is pretty light, it can take some wind, but not heavy winds. Taking the propeller guards off can help with this, but it's still a light weight drone, but great for beginners. It also comes with a housing for a GoPro or any standard sized action camera.

POST PRODUCTION SET-UP

Most people have what it takes to start up. The average computer can do editing. Start by reviewing your computer's specs. You want to be doing a minimum speed of 2 gigahertz and have at least 16 gigabytes of memory for best results dealing with 1080p video.

Wipe your computer clean of everything except important programs like MS Office (or iWork if you're on a Mac), Photoshop, screenwriting software and other needed programs. If you can buy a tablet for internet surfing versus using your computer, that too will help or only use trusted sites.

You will need software. If you are in school you can buy software, in some cases, at half price through certain companies. Install the software and get a fast external harddrive for your footage. The editing software will ask which drive to use to store the clips. You want a minimum of 1tb — 2tb of space for your clips and the render files that will go along with them for a feature film.

Non-Linear Editing Programs:

An NLE (Non-Linear Editing) **Program** will allow you to edit via taking clips you've shot, sound, photos, etc and inserting them where you want them to go. These are the big three:

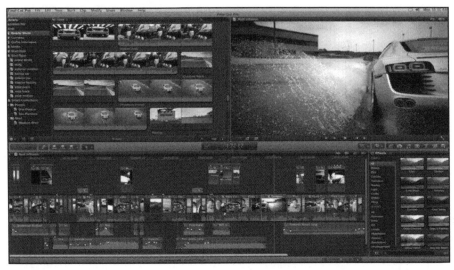

Final Cut Pro X: Okay, everyone knows I'm a Mac Addict. In 2011 Apple released Final Cut Pro X. While the program was long awaited, when it came to market a lot of people took to calling it "iMovie Pro." To the chagrin of pro users it lacked features pros used, like Multicam editing, support, EDL list and the big one, the inability to import Final Cut Pro projects while it could import iMovie projects.

While some resent Apple turning everything into an app, honestly I'd rather pay $300 for this than the original $800 for the program and $1000 for the suite. You can get FCPX and motion for $350 bucks and throw in compressor for a total of $400. You're still under $500. And who needs Soundtrack when you have GarageBand, which is better in my opinion.

While a lot of people didn't like the program it was still one of the most downloaded programs from Apple today. From a business standpoint here's what happened; Apple used iMovie to test what would indeed become Apple's new editing standard. iMovie ships with every new Apple and many people got use to using it. When they want to move up to a new more professional editor, they would probably buy Final Cut Pro X.

Personally I might have liked to see a Final Cut Pro 8 and an "iMovie Pro," but I'm willing to bet iMovie Pro would've eventually phased out Final Cut. Also a lot of complaints about the software came from people not really investigating the software, but simply seeing certain functions and assuming it wouldn't work the way they wanted it too. In the end, they were wrong. They simply didn't know how to assess the function they wanted.

But honestly, I like Final Cut Pro X. Many of the things "missing" I didn't use so I didn't have a problem. I keep hearing people who use the software to make money simply felt ripped off. But why wouldn't they simply keep using whatever version of FCP they had until they learned FCPX and caught up. I'll admit, it was new to me. When you have FCP you simply don't use iMovie. Now I wish I had used the latter versions of iMovie more.

To understand the new Final Cut you have to understand "File Based Editing". I'm sure you've heard this term before even if you don't know what it means. I'll give you a quick run down. Back in the day (just a few years ago) we would use digital tape to record footage and then ingest it like one would a basic video tape. This would actually shorten the life of the camera by wearing down the playheads, as most people used their camera to shoot and edit unless they had a deck or a cheaper camera to edit on (we had our original Panasonic palmcorder which we used as a deck for our DVX100).

Now editing is "file based," which mean every time you start and stop the camera a file is made, usually a .mov, m2t or MP4. The only moving part is the harddrive, if your camera is harddrive based and virtually none if your camera is card based, meaning it uses some kind of memory stick, P2 or the more common "SD" card to store the clips. It's faster and more convenient and you probably do it all the time. It was the norm with many consumer cameras, then quickly became a feature of pro cameras.

First off let's start with some new things. For the longest there were formats Apple simply didn't support natively, the most common being AVCHD files which are very common in modern filmmaking. FCP would transcode these to a better quality format for editing which was actually a good thing because it made for a higher quality edit. Now FCPX accepts these formats and will do any extra transcoding in the background. (When dealing with AVCHD files you have to import the whole folder from the camera). You can also begin to edit while files are being dropped into Final Cut Pro X.

One of the things that always irked me when editing with FCP (and many other programs) was the fact the audio and video could indeed get out of sync easily while editing if you're not paying attention. It's not so here. While it can happen, it's not as easy as with the old version because of how the audio is linked and the fact it moves out of the way when other audio may accidentally overlap it. The tradeoff is your have to learn how to work with audio all over again.

The program's ability to tell medium, longshots or close ups from one another is genius and the effects and integration with motion are very helpful. You can still import clips from Video CoPilot's "Action Essentials" and other things of that nature to do special effects right in the program. And while the keying maybe not be on the level of After Effects (especially with the "Keylight" plug in), you can get a pretty darn good key from it and look surprisingly professional. And it's certainly a lot better than iMovie's keyframer.

It's not perfect, as it can be a memory hog, uses events like iMovie does and honestly, I would prefer a "save" button on top of the autosave feature. But all and all I think it's a great piece of software. Take the time to learn this program as it doesn't take that long and there's tons of info online about it. People still scoff at it, but I believe it will become the future of file based editing. And with that being said, you can still edit from tape based DV and HDV cameras.

The reality is, it's not for everyone. If you're in a business where you need to know your system back and forth and you don't have time to learn something new, then you may want to check out the other programs! For the rest of us, this is everything Apple says it is. Overall cutting with this is a pleasure. Jumping between this and Final Cut 6 on my old desktop was such a stark contrast. I found myself longing for the ability to have the timeline split open to allow me to drop footage into certain places. But I'll also admit the old school cutting on the legacy FCP system still feels very comfortable. I'm still using it now currently on version 10.3.4 (it was 10.0.08 when I wrote the first edition) and they added a lot of stuff. And don't forget to download the free content including presets and over 1000 sound effects for FCPX.

Avid: These were big editing machines Hollywood used to use; now anyone can turn their computer into an Avid editing deck. This program can be pricey with all the trimmings, but many people in swear by it. A lot of people forgot about Avid, but it's still used and it's a standard in Hollywood. In the beginning this was the program that inspired Final Cut Pro, then changed to become more like Final Cut Pro, but  over time Avid still managed to hold on to an admirable fan base and in many schools both Avid and FCP are taught. At Columbia College here in Chicago FCP and Avid are both required for the Film/Television program. FCP is taught in the television department and Avid in the Film Department.

 **Premiere Pro:** Adobe Premiere was a huge name in Non-Linear Editing. Because of Photoshop and the "Adobe Suite" Premiere was a huge hit and had many supporters and fan, but over time it fell behind as Avid and Final Cut overtook the professional market. Premiere 6 would be the final release of the original Premiere system. In 2003 Adobe released Premiere Pro, a totally overhauled version of Premiere that functioned very much like FCP and Avid (I also taught Premiere Pro at a local college here in the city). You can still get this program in a suite for Mac or PC. The person who taught me FCP was a 3D animator who used the original Premiere for editing. After the release of Final Cut Pro X, many disgruntled Final Cut Pro users turned to Adobe Premiere because of its similarity with original FCP.

Premiere has a cheaper down and dirty editing program called Adobe Premiere Elements. Like Photoshop Elements, Premiere Elements is an inexpensive, no frills program that just gets the job done for people who can't afford Premiere Pro.

Sony Vegas (Originally Sonic Foundry's "Vegas Video"): I didn't throw this into my top three, but I want to be clear, that's only because Sony's marketing sucks in this area. Sony never took the initiative to push the program as a pro suite, but keeps it on the level of a consumer program. Vegas is a very capable program, one used mainly for wedding videography and such, but it can certainly handle movies, music videos and the like. If you're into Sony equipment and you're on a PC or Intel Mac running PC programs you may want to look at this NLE. One of the things about Sony Vegas is it's PC only. Because Apple itself, Avid and Premiere basically control the Apple Pro NLE market and since Macs come with iMovie, an advanced beginner program, a lot of people simply don't make Mac compatible NLEs as they consider it a waste of time and money.

Other Non-Linear Editing Programs:

Pinnacle Studio: Corel's editing software actually has a large cult following, in fact it claims to be the number one editing software. Some people love it. It's inexpensive, comes and three flavors, a $60 version, Pinnacle Studio for $100 and a pro version called Ultimate for $130 and now they've ended it's PC only exclusivity with an $8 app for the iPad, which may mean a Pinnacle Studio for Mac may be on the way which would awesome competition for Apple and possibly make way for even lower prices.

But the question is can you cut professionally on it and apparently the answer is yes, so much so Pinnacle was bought by Avid and then again, just this year purchased by software giant Corel. Pinnacle Studio isn't new, it's on it's 16th version. For an in depth look at it's differences and similarities you'd have to do your own research, but certainly it's an inexpensive and powerful software.

iMovie: This the free NLE that comes with all modern Apple Computers and was the testing floor for Final Cut Pro X. iMovie used to be a stripped down and very basic editor, totally different from Final Cut Pro, but now it's pretty powerful, in fact FCPX was based around iMovie's workflow. Now, people using iMovie can easily transition to Final Cut Pro X.

Some have stated that Apple should've created a new Final Cut Pro based on the legacy system and then created iMovie Pro as an app, but iMovie Pro probably would've overtaken Final Cut eventually and the move would've also went against what seems to be Apple's intention to streamline things.

Your Ambition Should Inform Your Need

As a Youtube producer you have to decide what it is you want to do. Are you going to be doing a talk show, game reviews or walk throughs, narrative TV or full length features. If you're reading this I'm sure you have some ideas already. But you should get the camera and equipment needed for your goals. Many cameras can be used for talks shows, but you may want something else for filmmaking or episodics.

WRITING AND BRAINSTORMING

The Youtube Model Versus the Old Model

As a Youtube producer you have some abilities you haven't had before, the ability to make movies or TV shows you know will air. And even IMDB will consider your Youtube show a TV show and will list your film if it's on Youtube, but the writing is different for each.

Comedy Shorts

These are pretty popular on Youtube. They're usually three to five minutes long and can be stand alone or continual episodes.

Features

As a partner you have unlimited space (just check out the ten hour loops). But for you, if your goal is youtube features you want to write for a minimum of seventy minutes. Some have done forty-five, but to standout as a feature seventy is good minimum and there is no maximum, it's all about your story and will people stick around for it. You can run one ad at the beginning, at the end, and maybe run an ad every ten minutes. With Epitaph: Bread and salt we ran an ad at the beginning and end and three in the middle so viewing would only be interrupted three time. Also, always remember to put the year of release, the kind of movie it is (action/horror/comedy) and the words "Full Movie" along with the movie's title in the title bar.

Documentaries

Docs aren't scripted, but planned. You would do a breakdown of where you're going and where you should be at specific times to meet the person you're going to interview. You should have a list of questions you plan to ask already to go. You'll have to video tape the person answering the questions and then turn the camera on yourself to show you asking the question. Depending on how you're structuring your documentary you may never even appear on screen. A good example of this is JR2 Films award winning documentary "Mound Bayou". Docs can be anywhere between ten minutes to ninety minutes or even longer.

How To's

"How To" is the most searched term on Youtube. Depending on what you're doing a "How To" can be anywhere from four to fifteen minutes or longer. People will watch if you're doing something they want to see. A big thing on Youtube, of course, is tech How To's, everything from taking a Macbook Pro apart, to making a DIY camera rig. In fact DIY projects are also very big.

Music Videos

This is your basic music video. This can be a professional music video or someone singing into a microphone. Covers are allowed, parodies are loved, but if you're an original artist a good video could be the start to fame and fortune. And for all the hate thrown at Rebecca Black, even her video was professionally produced. If you're doing your own you should learn how to make a pro video and watch other videos to see what shots are used, what looks you may like and then add your own creative flair. And you can shoot a 24 or 30p.

Serials

One thing to remember is Youtube is a place where people take in information in two to five minute bites. One of the things you're allowed to do is make serials. (Basically, a television show). The end of each show is a new revelation. A certain amount of shows are made and up loaded.

Because Youtube is different from television instead of once a week, you'd upload your show two to three times a week usually in four to seven minute chunks. Some shows do go from ten or fifteen minute chunks, but those are usually high drama, one example is the show "Lauren" on the WIGS network. WIGS is a network featuring shows by women about women. And most of the shows star celebrities like Troian Bellisario, Jennifer Beals and Julia Stiles. The shows are seven to ten minutes and even longer, with the longer ones usually being season or series finales.

Shopping Hauls
Like to shop? If you do you can show off and review the things you bought. A simply thing, but people love to see it.

Unboxing
Like the shopping haul you simply take the packaging off something you bought and show it off. This can be with or without a review, but should really have a review.

Walk Throughs
If you're playing a lot of video games, find some screen recording software, set it up and then simply play the game on your computer while you record it. A console system on the other hand needs a capture card to connect your console to your computer. There's plenty of tutorials for this on Youtube. While unscripted the key is good running commentary. Walk throughs can go anywhere from seven to fifteen and even thirty. Check out "TheRadBrad" Channel to see some good gaming and entertaining running commentary.

Commentary, Reviews and Vlogging
One of the issues with the first edition of this handbook is that I really aimed the book toward the Youtube filmmaker, but three of the main types of channels are: Commentary, Review and Vlogs. I went in depth about screenwriting, but not about these, which was a big oversight on my part. While they don't have a hard structure like a screenplay, there is a structure you can use that will make things a bit easier for you.

Opening and Ending: How are you going to open your videos and how are you going to end them? This could be as simple as "Hi guys" or "What's up everybody." If you already have an audience, "What's up (title of channel) fam?" You can end with , "Until next time..." or something like that, to get fans used to hearing you say it, a catch phrase and catchy music is a good idea too (see Using Music on Youtube in the "Editing and Post" section). Now that you have an opening and closing what are you going to do to fill that time in between...?

Commentary

If you're doing commentary, what are you going to talk about? Something that upset you that day? The political climate? Another Youtuber's channel? Your thoughts on modern entertainment? All of it's fair game, but remember, Youtube favors certain things and can limit ads or even demonetize your video (take away ad revenue) for things like swearing, talking about certain subject matter or simply being too edgy. While this is starting to happen less often, Youtube seeks content deemed "advertiser friendly". Things that most advertisers will have no issue with, so if you have a new commentary channel you've got to be on your toes all the time.

Reviews

If you're doing reviews, you're not completely out of the woods either. Some companies can't stand negative reviews and will come after you. If you do a review make sure any claims you make are well researched and factual and any opinion you have about a product based on those facts is just that, an opinion. This is generally low risk programming.

Vlogging

Vlogging is generally the safe bet. You're basically doing a video about what's going on in your life. It's mainly a highlight reel of your day. Your main challenge here is how to make it interesting. And since it's a vlog you're not tied down to any specific format, so one day you can do commentary, the next could be a review and then a shopping haul or unboxing, it's all up to you.

A sub-genre of vlogging is IRL (In Real Life) Streaming. IRL vloggers are typically streaming from their phone or a specialized streaming set up and you get to watch as they go through their day or do certain things. An IRL can take advantage of Youtube's streaming set up and get money from donations that come through Super Chats. Then the stream becomes a basic video and can be monetized. The problem with IRL is if people know where you are and can get there while you're streaming, they may interfere with the stream by harassing you, the people around you, or "Swatting" you (making false claims to the police to have them bring a SWAT team to your location).

Monday:

Shoot All Footage
Edit and Release Macbook Pro video

Tuesday:

Edit and Upload Vacation video
Edit Short Book Deal Video

Wednesday:

Upload Book Deal Video
Edit and Upload Car videos

Thursday:

Edit Endorsement Video
Edit Channel Commentary
Edit cooking video

Upload and Schedule Channel Commentary and cooking video for Friday and Saturday

Friday:
Start on next weeks videos. Shoot B-roll.

Brainstorming

Coming up with ideas can be a daily task. If you're going the quantity over quality route you're going to have to have something daily. For a commentator it's usually easier as there's always something in the news or online to discuss on your channel, but creating interesting content is a hard job, so this basic break down will help:

Topics

1. The New Macbook Book Pro
   a. How I feel about it.
   b. What are the design
   c. What are the design flaws
   d. Do I think it's worth the money?
   e. Will I get one?

2. My VacaEndorsementtion
   a. Where I'm going?
   b. What's my plan?
   c. Who I'm taking
   d. I will be vlogging

3. My New Book Club.
4. Talk about the car I want
5. The new endorsement
6. Why I really don't like that other channel.
7. How to cook cheesy potatoes
8. How to make knit a pot holder

1. Decide on the topic for the day or week. You can just flip through magazines, news feeds, the day's paper, watch news and other videos. List ideas that seem like you can make a solid video from.

2. If your content isn't time sensitive you can do multiple videos in a day and edit them through the week. This is good for instructional videos.

3. List the main points of what you want to say and where you want each point to go. This is important as it keeps you on track and helps stop rambling, but it's not an actual script.

3. Edit ASAP. Edit as soon as you can, don't let it become a chore. Or pick a day/time to edit.

4. Create and itinerary for editing and uploads so you will know what you're supposed to be doing that day.

5. If you're daily vlogging back up B-roll on a harddrive for later use.

Screenplays

Even for Youtube a screenplay is still needed and is still industry standard in feature and short filmmaking.

Three to five minutes seems to be the sweet spot for most videos, but then there are the feature filmmakers, making films between forty-five minutes to ninety minutes or more, as well as people making serials. You can find the bulk of this on the internet and there's no way I'm going to be able to truly cover screenwriting in a chapter in a book. You'll need an actual book on screenwriting.

A full length Youtube screenplay should be about seventy pages long. A good pro script is usually around 90 minutes. If you're shooting for yourself then you can make it whatever you want, but it should be at least 70 minutes. If you expect to try to sale a script for distribution go with 90 minutes, 105 or 120 max.

I'm going to list 10 basic things about a screenplay, but this is technical stuff not particularly structural.

1. A script is written in 12 point "Courier" (some programs have their own version of this font) on an 8 1/2 x 11 page (8.5 x 11).

2. The left margin is 1.5 inches, the right is 1 inch and that's because you will have to hole punch your script on the left when it's done, the top and bottom should be an inch. You should be able to set this up simply in Word, Apple Pages or whatever word processor word you have. But Celtx is free so get it.

3. **Scene Heading** (or the "Slugline") is the first. This sets up your location and time of day. It is in all caps and is formatted like so:

EXT. A NORTHSIDE JUNKYARD - DAY

EXT. means "exterior" and signifies a shot is taking place outside.

INT. is just the opposite and signifies a shot inside.

After the time of day is established you can simply write: "CON'T" as opposed to "DAY", "NIGHT", "EVENING", etc .

You have to use EXT. or INT. any time a scene changes because movies are shot out of order, so all the scenes are shot in one location at one time whenever possible. So this must be done every time a location changes.

4. **Action** is written in present tense formatted like so:

```
With the wooden stake raised. He stands at the door but
doesn't enter. He glances around the corner. Diana sits
perched on the fifth floor balcony.
```

Action is everything that happens during a scene. Everything you want to happen in this shot should be in the description. Be brief, but get all the important details in. Try to limit it to three or four lines, five max. I personally tend to break mine up to three line paragraphs if I need to put a lot in.

5. **Character Name** is exactly what it says. Two things you have to know about character names. The first time a new character is introduced their name is capitalized (see example below).

```
NATHAN MATTHEWS a thuggish looking man, with corn-rolled hair,
wearing a black collared shirt and pants set with a black
leather trench coat walks down the street. He notices a red
car and stops in his tracks.
```

Their name is also capitalized whenever they talk to alert the actor who is when they should speak.

6. **Dialogue** is set apart from the rest of the action 2.9 inches from the left of the page is standard and it goes beneath the character name:

BIG BUSINESS
How's it hanging Johnny?

NATHAN
How's it hanging? You got work or what?

BIG BUSINESS

```
          Work? You're a trigger man Johnny, but you
          can't seem to kill anybody. All your marks
          seem to end up in witness protection.
```

Don't use caps, bold, or italics when writing dialogue, underscore the text you want to emphasize.

7. **Parentheticals** are special actions placed in parenthesizes normally for the speaking actor to describe how the actor should move, feel or gesture. They go under the Character name or to the right and are usually some kind of adjective:

```
                    NATHAN
                   (calmly)
          I don't know what you think you
          know but we can talk about this.
          Let me talk to Mr. Constantine -
```

Just so you know, this is frowned upon. It's the director's job to direct and the actor's job to act. The script should speak for itself, but sometimes it can be useful, but use it sparingly.

8. **Extensions** (not be confused with parentheticals) denote how a person is being heard (OS) is very common and usually means "Off Screen…"

```
          BUSINESS CLASS (O.S.)
       Mr. Constantine says you're out.
```

9. **Transition** are how shots move from one to the other. The most used transition is a "CUT". Some scenes FADE OUT while others FADE IN. Sometimes a scene will "WIPE" or "DISSOLVE." The transition goes on the right and is only noted if it's something other than a cut or if it's a specific cut and it's in all caps and to the right like so...

```
                                        CUT TO:
```

```
Four men moving through the entrance of the junk yard and two
other moving in on Nathan from behind cars loading guns.
```

10. A **Shot** is what is in frame from the time the camera is rolling until the camera stops. And all the shots that take place in one location at one specific time on screen, pertaining to one specific event is your **scene**.

Now that you got that down you're already on your way to writing a script. The technical elements can be tedious, that's why it's good to have a screenwriting program, but back in college Microsoft Word, Word Perfect and MacWrite/Claris were all we had.

Other tidbits you may want to know are people don't come or go they either "enter" or "exit". Entering and exiting denote coming into the frame or leaving it. Any time there is a specific sound effect you should capitalize the sound effect in the script.

```
Nathan takes off running as the men FIRE at him. He exits as
they give chase.
```

The reason for this is it helps calculate cost (squibs, explosions and "bullet hits" cost money) and tells the sound person what sounds he needs to be preparing for the film.

So now you have a basic breakdown of what a screenplay is and how to format it. A poorly formatted screenplay will get you booted in a minute. Again if you're writing for yourself you have some space to play around, but remember this format is designed that each page equals a minute of screen time and it normally works out that way, so even if you're doing your own film this works to your advantage. This is what it should look like:

```
INT. ANOTHER PART OF THE JUNKYARD - DAY

NATHAN MATTHEWS  a thuggish looking man, with corn-rolled
hair, wearing a black collared shirt and pants set with a
black leather trench coat looks at his cellphone clock.
BUSINESS CLASS, a tall stocky man and BRIAN, a slender Asian
man enter from behind a junk stack.

                        BUSINESS CLASS
```

How's it hanging Johnny?

                    NATHAN
How's it hanging? You got work or what?

                    BUSINESS CLASS
Work? You're a trigger man Johnny, but
you can't seem to kill anybody. All your
marks seem to end up in witness protection.

                    NATHAN
                    (calmly)
I don't know what you think you, let me
talk to Mr. Constantine -

                    BUSINESS CLASS (O.S.)
Mr. Constantine says you're out.

                                        CUT TO:

Four men entering through the entrance of the junk yard and
two others moving in on Nathan from behind cars loading guns.

Nathan takes off running as the men FIRE at him.

INT. ANOTHER PART OF THE JUNKYARD - DAY

Junk is piled high. Nathan enters and leaps behind the pile,
rolls and snatches two 9mm pistols from under his coat then
runs out from behind the junk barrier firing at the on coming
attackers as they return fire.

Structure

Structure is the next focus and this is important. Scripts have a three act structure, which I will break down to: **Beginning, Middle,** and **End.** I'll get more specific on this, but what you need to know is what's called the "**Three Act Structure**".

Now you don't have to follow this structure, some screen plays are done in four or five acts where either the beginning middle or end are elongated into multiple acts. If you're looking to sell a script the three act structure is expected. Hollywood has it's rules and if you don't have millions of dollars they normally won't break those rules for you, then again if you had millions of dollars you wouldn't need Hollywood or this book.

An **Act** is normally one-third of your film broken down into Act 1: **The Set Up**, Act 2: **Confrontation** and Act 3: **Resolution**.

The Set Up or **Exposition:** Is what is says. This will drive the movie and everything from this point on will have to do with the set up. You will introduce the audience to your characters and how they relate to one another.

This is has to be the strongest part of the story as it is what will pull people into your movie or not, whether it's an action film, romance or comedy this is what will make your audience want to continue watching. This is where **Dramatic Premise** and **Dramatic story** come into play and it should be done within about five to ten minutes.

The **Dramatic Premise** is basically what the whole movie is about **Dramatic Story** or **Situation** are the specific set of circumstances that move things along. Then there is what I call the **First Domino** or **Inciting Incident** which is the first specific action that happens to push the story into high gear.

In "The Fourth Beast" the premise was and Ex-Army Ranger is given a CD with information about the Antichrist and he has to get that CD to a waiting journalist while avoiding rogue Vatican Intelligence Agents.

The Dramatic Situation is Daniel (Jon Ross' character), has just gotten back from Iraq. He wants to get back together with his old girlfriend whose also military but didn't go back. Obviously him getting this disc and being tracked by these "agents" gets in the way of his desire for love.

The first domino happened very late in the film (not good) which was the Daniel being attacked in the park by the agents and their posse. One could argue the first domino was when Daniel's friend, a priest he knew from high school, was killed. But I'd say, if Daniel isn't attacked, we don't have a movie.

In "Wages" the premise is Johnny Trigger, a supposed hitman, is found out to be an undercover cop. So the bad guys put a price on his head which of course leads to assassins coming after him.

The story is: After watching a drug dealer kill one of his partners during an undercover operation officer Matthews wants to know how the investigation got botched. From the way it looks to him someone on the inside is dirty. He wants to find out who it is and take the drug dealers down. To do this he has to avoid a hot, but deadly female assassin, hit squads and other supposed law enforcement agents.

Teresa our reluctant hooker character, ends up being the leading lady who helps him get the evidence to nail the bad guy. She has a "dramatic story" of her own. She hates being a hooker, juxtaposed to her friend who loves the life. Teresa ends up getting the evidence of an unrelated crime committed by the main bad guy.

The first domino could be looked at as the shooting of his partners, but since the movie is based around his current actions the first domino will be his being attacked in witness protection by a rogue FBI agent which, of course, leads to him having to leave witness protection and fend for himself.

Many low budget screenplays are usually what's called derivative, meaning they were based on or are like something that was already out there. This doesn't mean they have to be, a lot just are. *"The Fourth Beast"* was my own concept while the *"Wages of Sin"*, was inspired by Jet Li's "Kiss of the Dragon" yet it is obviously very different. I took the idea of a good cop being preyed upon by bad ones and re-worked it in my own low-budget way.

Act two is **The Confrontation** which is when all the problems are thrown at our hero or heroine that they have to over come to get through to the third act. Here the character meets the assassins, bad guys, or whoever their antagonist is either face to face or via their goons or representatives. This is usually the longest part of the movie.

Act three is the **Climax, Resolution, Final Conflict** or whatever you want to call it. This is where the problem gets solved or the problem is left unresolved, which is happens sometimes in dramatic movies, but even then it's not left unresolved as much as the resolution is unspoken. In the film "Secret Lies", a freak accident leads to the main character finding out their spouse is committing adultery.

The resolution doesn't at all feel like a resolution, but we understand what it probably means about the characters. We question what the future may hold as nothing is spelled out for the viewer. And if you want to know what happens to the characters then that's a sign of good writing as it shows you were actually interested in their lives and their stories.

Writing for Budget

It's simple, be realistic. Considering your "budget" is very important for a micro-cinema. You cannot do "The Matrix" on a $1000 budget. I take that back, if you have people willing to work with you, the time and someone to loan you sets, props etc you can do something Matrix-like.

Special Effects Limits

A lot of the effects from big films can be done in some form or fashion at home now on a laptop computer with "After Effects" or "Shake". But you're going to have to decide what you can and can't do based on your budget, time and talent.

When I did *"Wages of Sin"* I knew it would be a cheesy action film with heartfelt platitudes, but it was what I've always wanted to do — one of my dream projects and so much fun. I understood my budget and didn't try to go beyond it like I did the first time.

It's awesome when people tell me "I liked your film!" or "I really enjoyed your movie" and say it like they mean it. I can tell people were humoring me during the first film because even I knew it wasn't great. (But it was better than a lot of other stuff on the market according to some, based solely on the story). But we didn't go for any big explosions or massive car chases. We based everything on martial arts, a few gunfights and story, and for the most part, it worked.

Most low budget companies have access to After Effects and a green-screen. This will open the door to many effects in itself, but they may not have access to high end stuff like *Maya* or other comparable 3D modeling and animation programs; and if you do, do you know how to use them effectively as there's a reason people are paid big money for this kind of thing. Even if you don't have this stuff let's not forget about old school practical effects. They work and are still used in many horror films.

The reason I bring all this up is if you're doing this all on your own you better know what you're capable of and what you're not. If you don't know how to G-Screen a remote controlled helicopter and drop it into a scene (or don't know anyone who can) don't write it into the script. The most simple effects are gun shots, blood sprays and bullet hits, though Lasers are becoming big too, but write only what you have access to.

Location Limits
Again when writing a script many think about it from a Hollywood standpoint, palatial estates, big explosions and car chases — that all cost money. If you're writing romance, your film will sale on romance, if you're writing a thriller your film will sale on thrills, if you're writing action and you don't have explosions and gun fights then you better have tons of awesome martial arts and chase scenes. That's all you really need, that and a decent story.

First you decide what your budget is. This will decide your script. When I was in film school there was a restaurant called "The Harrison". It was on Harrison Street right next door to Columbia College. We ate there all the time and they were very open to us poor film students.

Eventually, "Chicago Carry Outs" bought out The Harrison. Chicago Carry Out was a fast food place that sold "Hot Dogs Specials" for $1.99 (I think eventually went up to $3.99). The HDS was a hotdog, fries and a drink. Very basic, but the fries were good if nothing else. They were also very nice to us. I made it a point to shoot a least one scene in The Harrison/Chicago Carry

Outs for all my projects, until they finally closed their doors. It was a free location and I could feed my team cheap.

This is forward thinking. Every location you can get for free needs to end up in your film, so budget and write around this. That's why many low budget movies consist of alleys, grease shacks and underground parking garages. This is stuff they can get for free or cheap. If you have a lot of contacts who have nice apartments, homes and warehouses (industrial spaces) then you're in luck, otherwise you'll have to limit it to the places you know you can get. That's how it's done. Once you have a bunch of free locations, you can literally write your screenplay based on them.

Location Scouting
If you're not working with a big budget you don't have the luxury for high-end location scouting unless you know somebody.

First off what makes a good location? Old places, like libraries or book stores that deal in "used" books, hotels, older school buildings (specifically colleges), alleys, fashionable or upscale neighborhoods, club districts, rooftops, parks, downtown streets at night, upscales offices, etc.

These all make for good locations and many times were free. When we did the *"The Fourth Beast"* all of the locations were free. How did we get them? We asked. We used a nice bookstore (it's closed now), Chicago Carry-Outs again, Grant Park, two actors' apartments, Columbia College and their dorms, the dorm gym, the alley by the dorms (used in *"Wages of Sin"* also) and the street by the dorms.

So how does one location scout? Grab a camera, a nice digital camera is a blessing, but a basic disposable camera would do just fine. Go to places you know you can get for free and snap photos. Get all the nook and crannies.

You want to also use the photos so you'll have some idea of what your blocking will be. The blocking for Chicago Carry Outs was easy. I know the very simple, layout, but blocking for the two room safehouse was on the fly because I'd only seen it once and didn't have photos. The woman who rented us the storefront knew the landlord and connected us up.

I did a very quick walk through. We were lead through the back and went out the front. I liked the place, especially the old stairwell, but had no real idea how to incorporate it, even though a basic walk down did the trick. I didn't even think about how to block and shoot the scene until we broke it down on set that day because the room was basically barren.

Riti, our resident butt-kicking Bollywood babe, had gotten into a bit of a snag so she was running late. This worked out because it gave me time to consider how things were going to go. I had Richard Lang one of my camera operators there and Alan Serrano, fielding the roles of boom operator and grip for the day. We talked for a bit and I got a chance to really look at the place, and even used the balcony.

The last part of this scene would end with Mona Lisa, the main badgirl, being shot by Hokkaido Clan accountant turned avenger, Max Hokkaido, played by model/actor Tonee Dang. That scene was done already so once we shot this safehouse fight we could connect the scenes up.

The Columbia fight went a lot smoother. Again I knew the location and knew what I wanted. It was yet another stairwell. I knew I wanted someone to leap over the banister and into the fight and for Shawn had to do a kick off the wall, I knew without a shadow of a doubt I wanted those two dynamic actions in this stairwell. I hatched it out. In my head I saw what the fight should look like. After meeting with Shawn, a competent choreographer in his own right, he added something else, rapid punches and a sweep maneuver.

I was a grounded fighter, but Shawn was an all around kung fu king. So I did blocks and redirects. A lot of it, while not specifically Aikido, was based on Steven Segal movies, versus Shawn's Jet Li-esque moves.

In this scene I would lose the fight, so Shawn was just the man to make this work the way I saw it in my head. My character was a cop, who knew martial arts, not a "martial arts cop" like you see in so many films. Shawn's character was an enforcer. His living was made from being able to beat somebody down if needed. Tonee Dang would be the stair jumper and our original cameraman, Jin Ho Kim, who also did double duty portraying Richard Hokkido, had the hard job of looking on with approval or disapproval as his guys fought me.

This was one of those move out on faith type situations. I went into this scene, but didn't really have any props aside from two batons, which had been used in the film already and a stage knife. I knew what I wanted, but mulled over what I could do to create the same effect with what I had. Everything changed when I went upstairs to get the safety mats and went to the wrong floor.

The elevator opened and I walked into a massive brawl that started from the elevator bay and ended at the last classroom on the fourth floor. People had daggers, knives and sticks. They were beating the crap out of each other, doing flips, leaps and kicks. I had never seen anything like this in real life. Welcome to Columbia College's Staged Combat Department. I new it existed, but had never seen it. I'd only met one instructor and just once in my life. My heart was emboldened. These were my people. I walked directly to the office and told them my plight. They checked me out and within moments I signed out the knives we used in the hallway scene. And these were professional props, no plastic crap. If you've seen the film you know how the scene turned out.

Budgeting and X-Factors
The next thing is make sure the script is something that can be accomplished. I'm assuming you're a one person show or maybe have a little backing from friends and family or even a few nice investors.

Actors and crew don't want to waste time on something that won't get made and cost can become a huge obstacle. Factor in transportation, time and what you're going to need outside of the shoot. The biggest cost for me was transportation and food. (Food can run from $20 to $50 a day).

Food is important on any shoot. If you've got a crew that's working for free the least you can do is feed them. The crew expects pizza, Chinese food, cheese burgers and/or hotdogs and fries. Energy drinks and Gatorade ("Gator-juice") or Powerade all come in handy so budget all this in. You'll also need to know who will get paid (if anyone) and who won't. We paid our lead actors by the day. It wasn't much, but they knew I wanted to pay and wasn't just trying to use their talents for free. Other actors didn't get paid, but were only used once or twice and we tried to make their time pleasurable so it all worked out.

Now that you have this all figured out and your script outline is done you need to find a cheap graphic designer. You should know (or learn) Photoshop. If you don't know it get someone to do a poster for you. If you don't have actors someone can piece together a cover symbolic of what your movie is about.

Character Limits

Yes, you can write a screenplay with a lot of characters in it or you can write one with three majors and everyone else is a window character or extra. In fact in a script with five characters, I'd say two should be absent for much of the time or there should be major focus shifting.

One thing to remember is the audience will only connect with no more than three characters (and that's pushing). And you will probably not have time to fully develop more than two. In *"Wages"* we already talked about our three, but even in a drama the main characters are the most developed as they're the ones you'll be following for most of the film.

In *"Wages of Sin"* we focused on Detective Matthews, he was our protagonist, Teresa and Jazz were the two working girls. These three characters took up most of the screen time. Then Jazz had an unfortunate incident and it was just Matthews and Teresa. Almost every major scene involved Matthews or Teresa. There was a subplot with Tonee and Riti's characters. They got a few scenes, but they were very quick. This was a budget consideration as I wanted them to do a longer martial arts too but it just didn't happen.

One of the reasons horror films are so cheap is because the killer kills characters off. The characters are only there until they're dead. Plus there's a lot of isolation. You can shoot with one actor on one day and get tons of footage and then send them home for the rest of the shoot.

You'd get group shots on days when everyone is available then from there only get shots with the important cast members, then edit it all together in the proper order. But once you have all the scenes where everyone or more than three are together you can start your isolation.

So when you're writing think about how you're going to be isolating characters and how you'll be moving between scenes. Where will isolated characters be and where will groups be? It's better to get groups in locations you know you can get for long periods of time (particularly for free). Isolated scenes can be in places where you may have to be rushed out of or may be paying for by the hour or day. Factor all of this in.

Scene Limits

Scenes should be no more than about three to five minutes (five at the longest)unless something so dynamic is taking place it warrants a long scene. This is done to keep things moving and to keep people's attention spans. But I say this knowing that there are episodics and shorts that have been nothing but one long scene, the HBO show *"In Treatment"* comes to mind. It's mostly dialogue and is built mainly on good acting.

The thing is most microbudget movies will not have great actors and if they do they won't have great directors. I used to come from the school of "Actors act, right?" Meaning once they read the script they should know what to do with minimal direction, but this is wrong headed thinking. Actors do "act" but a director needs to "direct". Tell the actors, how you see the scene playing out.

With this in mind, try to keep dialogue short, crisp and to the point. Tell the story with actions as much as possible. Sometimes dialogue is needed, make it strong enough and engaging enough that we want to know what's being said. Nothing's worse than a boring dialogue scene that goes on way too long.

Audiences are disengaged in several ways, one being repetitious dialogue. A character doesn't need to repeat things to the same person in different ways unless the person is a child or simply lacks basic understanding.

Another way audiences are disengaged is through "boring tripe." That's dialogue that doesn't mean anything, is slow and/or doesn't move the story forward. Cut this stuff down to the bare minimum. All dialogue should be interesting and move the story forward in some way.

What makes a good story?

This is a good question and while some may, I will make no attempt to answer such a subjective question. The only thing I would say is whatever draws the viewer into the story is what makes it "good".

Different stories are good for different reasons. An action film with a decent plot, reasonable pacing and great action will be deemed "good". A scary horror film will be deemed "good" a romance that made you cry or feel something for the characters is deemed as "good" and so on. Instead of saying what makes a story good, I'll say what ever story needs:

Conflict

Every good story has a battle between good, evil, right, wrong or one way versus the other. In every good story someone wants something and someone wants something else that opposes the main character. In a film like "Terminator 2" the conflict is obvious. The protagonists want to live and the new Terminator wants them dead.

Sometimes conflicts aren't so direct. In a film two people could have two totally different goals that don't really conflict, but they're bought into opposition as they go about achieving thing. Example right off the top of my head:

A cop is seeking a way to shut down the mob and an actor is seeking to be the next big thing in Hollywood. These seem to be two different events, but if that actor gets involved in a movie that happens to be backed by the mob then there could be conflict. Now suppose the actor is the cop's son or daughter.

Conflict comes in many different flavors: Conflict between the protagonist and antagonist as well as conflict with people around them who are not particularly antagonist but are "antagonistic" to the main character. There can even be conflict between secondary characters or even side conflicts. Imagine if you will two people who dislike each other, but their spouses are best friends with the other person's spouse. So you have conflict between the main characters and between them and their spouses. Good movies are built on this kind of tension. If you get this down, no matter what the budget you'll be able to make a great story.

The best struggle is between good and evil. But these are really abstracts. We use general ideas of what we believe to be good versus those we see as evil. Take "world domination". We assume in most films that if someone wants to dominate the world that will be a bad thing, but how do we know? The perception is if someone wants to dominate the world they are greedy and power hungry, which these characters usually turn out to be.

Another example, a cop who knows martial arts. If he catches a bad guy and gets a little rough with him because we automatically assume that this guy is a good guy and we excuse certain things from them that would make a real cop guilty of "excessive force" or "brutality". Ironically there's a Thomas Ian Griffith film called *"Excessive Force"* about a tough renegade cop who cleans up the street. Yes, he's a "loose canon" and all those good things we love and expect from our action hero cops except those played by Jet Li.

A good story is also based on point of view. If a viewer has a "Liberal" view and the story champions conservative values they may not like it. If the viewer is "Conservative" and the movie champions Liberal values they may not like this. But being able to surpass views and beliefs and make people feel for the character is what good writing is all about.

All you can do is make what is good to you and hope others will like it. Ask yourself this question: Would I buy or rent this? Knowing what I know about my own work I think I can honestly say I would rent "The Fourth Beast" but buy *Wages of Sin*.

I like the concept of *"The Fourth Beast"* more but, *"Wages of Sin"* has better production values, more action and a lot of other qualities I'd want in a film. Be honest with yourself. Is it really up to par?

Getting back to conflict even a romance has conflict. While usually non-violent the conflict maybe be between one person who wants more from a relationship and the other person who doesn't want the relationship to go further or simply hasn't thought of the first person in the same manner. The best romances start off with the people being either totally different and always bickering, but in the end "love" brings them together.

Starting up and ending are the hardest parts. You have to make a story that immediately sucks people in and then ends strong. No matter what kind of story you're telling you need to give the watcher reason to care about your character or the situation they're in. I try to start off each story with something that immediately make someone ask "why?" and make them sit through the film to find out. It's a tactic I use in many stories including novels. Sometimes it's simpler than that, just having a person doing something interesting will suck people in; the original *"Ghostbusters,"* does this all too well.

Types of Conflict

There are several different kinds of conflict, many of them are very common and you've probably heard of some, if not all them. Most people who've done any sort of study in screenwriting have come across the five types:

Man versus Fate: Basically you know it's coming, whatever *it* is, and the protagonist has to fight it. It's not as common as the rest but, *Final Destination* is a great film that takes man versus fate to a whole new level by personifying death. Can a person escape death again if they're destined to die and actually "escape" it a first time? Since death is the destiny of all living creatures the trick is delaying the inevitable as long as possible.

Fate, of course, is the belief things are slated to play out in a certain way no matter what choices you make. Somehow a character finds out their "fate" and makes decisions to either change it and either *do* change it or find their decisions are actually a part of "Fate's" ultimate plan. Another film that examines this is "The Number 23" or "23" as it's called, starring Jim Carrey in a great dramatic role.

Man versus Man: Probably the most common in action and genre films both the protagonist and antagonist are present and do battle in some form or fashion, either through kicking butt and taking names or outwitting one another in various ways until one person wins the conflict.

Man versus Nature: You see this in disaster films where a flood is coming that no one can stop or a comet is racing toward the earth or either for some reason the earth is about to go through another ice age or even something as basic a someone letting a bunch of snakes lose on a plane. Whatever the deal the protagonist will have to deal with the natural disaster generally by stopping it or escaping from it while, most times, having to rescue a family member, significant other, pet, or whatever in the process. And sometimes there's another antagonist to take on in the process.

Man versus Self: Alcoholism, drug addiction, sex addiction, etc are all common forms of man versus self. Addiction and other psychological or moral battles that play out where a person has to decide between something they want, but know they shouldn't have, are man versus self. The protagonist has to make a choice to "do the right thing" normally with the alternative choice being either self destructive or harmful to others.

This can be hard to work with because the only way we see the battle is by the main character's actions and by how the window character or characters are effected. The acting has to be good.

Man versus Society A character faces off with social conventions and either wins or is shown why the convention is right or works. Normally society equates to government, Church, PTA Boards or any given group considered to be "authority". This is popular now especially with society leaning toward a more relative morality.

Considering one person can't fight society (except in action films and even then there's an organization that represents "society") an antagonist will usually embody "society" meaning they will express views and such that said "society" holds. The protagonist is looked at as the underdog being oppressed, fighting for individuality and freedom.

Character Driven Stories

As mentioned before in a character driven story characters consistently make decisions that move the story along. Action films are usually plot driven. Most stories have both character and plot elements to them, but what really drives the story is what we see active the most. *"The Matrix"* was plot driven, but there are some character driven moments. Neo had to decide to take the red pill. He was given the choice, but up until that point he was being forced to make decisions because of the situations he was being put in. After making *the choice* he was again forced to make decisions based on the situation.

Character Generation

Before computers took over people played tabletop RPGs (Role Playing Games). *Dungeons and Dragons* was the most known, but there were (and are) many, many others, *Champions* probably being one of the best. Each game has its own character creation or *generation* system. In your screenwriting it can become a challenge mapping out your characters, so "generate" them.

In microbudget movie making characters can easily come out to be two dimensional. Why? Because most times low budget films aren't well thought out. They're built on a concept, but don't go far beyond that. You read about character limits, so you should be only developing a maximum of three characters. Ask yourself these five questions:

1. Who is this character?

This encompasses who they are, where they hail from, why they act and speak the way they do and why they do what they do. Easy go-to things would be a victim of child abuse, may themselves be abusive. A female character with no father will gravitate toward any man the shows her affection, particularly an older man. A character who was abandoned as a child may be clingy.

Reading psychology books will help in this area. You need to answer questions like: Why do they drink? Why do they engage in risky sexual behavior? Or why are they morally strict? Are there dichotomous, like being a cop, but engaged in some form of criminal activity, such as drug use or are they religious, but commit adultery or have premarital sex? If so, why are they doing this? Do they feel it's wrong? Are they trying to stop?

Is the character *"hard headed"* such as a victim of lung cancer continuing to smoke, or not listening to good advice such as that given by a good friend when they know a bad outcome is on the horizon.

Understanding why your character does what they do will be most helpful. The character should move themselves, not be wholly controlled by the writer. And sometimes we may never know why a character is the way they are but you as the writer should know.

2. What are their signatures?
I have a character that tends to put gum in his mouth every time he's about to have a face to face with someone. He's cocky and also uses the word "indeed" a lot. I have another that blatantly lies about things when they feel they're in some kind of trouble and after a deal is done he'll ask "you good?"

These are signatures. Every bit as good as James Bond's catch phrase *"Shaken not stirred"* or *"Bond. James Bond..."* they vary the characters up. Each main character should have their own speech, patterns of behavior and thought processes (which can only be shown by their actions). Little things like this can mean a lot. Remember, characters need to be fully developed.

3. What do they want?
What is the character's main goal? What are they trying to accomplish (or stop someone else from accomplishing). Not simply just "he wants to get the girl," but why does he want to get the girl? And why that particular girl? The normal answer is *"He loves her,"* or *"He wants to be loved,"* which may be good enough, but even that can be further explored.

4. How far?
How far will a character go to achieve their goals. Will they fight? Will they die? Or will they simply turn and walk away? This should be based on the first question. As an example a passive aggressive character doesn't suddenly decide to confront their significant other when they find out the significant

other is constantly sleeping over their ex's house, but they may *accidentally* wash a favorite color shirt in bleach or "accidentally" do something to their property in their absence. They will take round about ways to get forms of revenge, or answers, but not confront the main problem until they're forced.

5. Do they change?

The main character should change by the end of the film. A hardened character may become softer, an evil person my become good or even heroic. The big change normally happens to the main character. *"Collateral"* is a great example as Jamie Foxx 's character, Max changes as he has to deal with various situations that Vincent (Tom Cruise's character), keeps getting him mixed up in.

Max was lightweight, the kind of guy that wouldn't lift a finger to make a dream come true, but would fantasize about it all the time. By the end of the film he makes some heroic moves to save a woman he just met. He changes.

Character Growth

The protagonist must grow. As a film goes on the character should learn something and change. This is done over time. The character needs to realize something that makes them gain new insights. This growth comes from the character going through a situation and realizing they've come out of it stronger or better or sometimes they just came out of it alive. They learn they need to spend more time with their family, so they say *"no"* to the boss some time, or maybe they need to learn not to judge a book by its cover or any number of things they can come away with.

Types of Characters

Protagonist are NOT specifically the "good" guys. I had to impress this on my students all the time. If I ask on a test, "What is a protagonist?" and they answer "the good guy" I will mark it wrong every time. Yes, most times the protagonist is the "good guy" but is Chev Chelios a good guy? No, not really. A protagonist is simply the person whose story we're following throughout the tale.

Most of the time the protagonist should be on screen. We may get glimpses into what others are doing, but most of the scenes should deal with what the protagonist is doing. This is the person you want your audience to connect with. This is person who should be most developed and most defined.

Antagonist are NOT the "bad" guys. They're simply the person in the way of the protagonist getting what they want. Think about this from the perspective of an interracial love story. The antagonist could be family or friends (not particularly bad people) who stand in the way of two people getting together simply because they're of different races.

The antagonist is the person you want your audience to NOT side with, even if they have a reason why they feel or do what they do. Antagonist should also have a lot of development, and at times they may even be sympathetic.

Window Characters are characters that help reveal things about the main character usually via conversations with the main character or others about the main character. Max's mom was a window character in *"Collateral"*. Sometimes a best friend, close relative or even priest are used to fill this space.

Canon Fodder are usually guys standing around waiting for some action hero, monster, psycho killer, (or some big space alien if they happen to be wearing a red shirt on the Enterprise) to beat them up, eat them up or tear them apart.

Canon fodder characters can actually get a little development. There's always a few who stand out from the rest, especially when it comes to bad guys in actions films, as there's always one who you like the best because of their look, the way the act or something they do that endears you slightly to them.

Plot Driven Stories
Plot driven stories are just the opposite. The character makes decisions based on what's going on around them. As stated many action films and some episodic television shows are plot driven.

Plot Devices

A plot device is a technique used to move the story along and force the character move in specific ways and make specific choices. There are the three major ones.

Deus ex machina is when something totally unforeseen resolves the problems for the protagonist. This creates the ability for the story to end, usually, happily. This can be anything from that person everyone thought was dead coming back and taking out those bad guys the hero couldn't get to, or said ex-dead person freeing the hero right before they die in a tragic way, to divine intervention or a freak accident.

The phrase "deus ex machina" is Latin and comes from the Greek theater. A mechane (or crane) would lower actors playing a god or gods onto the stage at the end of a play and they would fix the problems.

The thing to remember here is the school of thought that says the protagonist is to solve the problem, so *deus ex machina* should only be used as an aid to the protagonist and not the final solution *unless* the final solution is somehow implied therefore probable and makes sense.

In the film "Dracula 2000," Dracula was taken out with a little divine intervention, but considering the plot of the film surrounded vampires, Dracula specifically and considering what we know about him and crosses this made sense. If the "machina" isn't set up in someway at the beginning then it obviously comes off as hack writing.

MacGuffins are any person place or thing which push the characters to do something, but the actual nature of the object is not important to the story. That means if you swap out that object for something else, most times the story would still work. Alfred Hitchcock, was famous for using MacGuffins.

MacGuffins have been around for years such as in many mythological tales where a character goes after an object. Sure the object doesn't do anything specific but the point is how the hero gets to the object and gets through whatever barriers are placed their to stop him or her in the process. The

Maltese Falcon is the most famous example of a MacGuffin. What does the Maltese Flacon do? Why was it so important? Anyone know? Nope.

Peripeteia is a plot device like Deus ex machina but, comes from figuring things out, such as catching on to something a character does that exposes their weakness and quickly turns the tide for the protagonist.

DC comics' beloved Batman character is great for this. Batman always deduces something and stops the badguy based on what he's figured out. In one story, DC's *Justice League* were being demolished by a group of alien super beings. Batman knew he couldn't fight them head to head, but through research and deduction Batman concluded these beings were Martians, (like his friend and JLA leader, Martian Manhunter). This turned the tide, as in the DCU (DC Universe) Martians are afraid of fire, so Batman started burning things around them. As powerful as these villains were they, indeed, turned out to be Martians and afraid of fire. Tide turned real quick that day.

Subplots

Basically the subplot is what's going on with the main or another character(s) as the main story is being told. To keep things ordered, the subplot should have something to do with the actual main plot otherwise it can be more distracting than interesting.

One thing about the subplot is to make it interesting it has to be fully developed just like the plot. This will involve covering your bases and keeping track of everyone involved more than normal.

Many screenplays today don't have a subplot. They focus on the main character and that's all. But one movie that comes to mind is *"Requiem for a Dream,"* which has several on going subplots all linked together by the Jared Leto character, Harry Goldfarb. Each person has a relationship with him and each person in some way, shape or form was addicted to drugs. And they all have big dreams.

In *"Requiem"* Harry and his friends were heroine addicts, but his mother was hooked on diet pills (and apparently game show based infomercials) that generally had the same effect as speed thanks to a shady doctor. Each person had their own story, but in the end it was all one story about each person's downfall due to drugs.

The movie *"Go"* also had intertwining subplots that all came together in the end. *Pulp Fiction* is a major film with great subplots. Not only did these films have engrossing subplots they were all very good movies.

Writing Dialogue

Remember, you're doing a low budget film so be smart about dialogue. For me I love to hear what characters have to say and I love to write dialogue but the dialogue shouldn't be telling the story. Writer/Producer John H. Rogers III, whose helped me out a few times, says one should think about what a character is saying, and if that can be shown as opposed to said, show it.

I had a character talking to his wife about why he was going to divorce her. John said, "She knows what she's doing. We know what she's doing. Why doesn't he just give her the papers?" Another scene I had the main character say, "The refrigerator's full of food." In response to his wife leaving to get groceries at an odd hour. Again John noted, the character just opened the refrigerator and we all saw it stocked with food. This eventually became a story I'm using for a novel, but I still used these suggestions and it made the story stronger. To write good dialogue sometimes you have to *not* say things. What you want to consider is, do the things your characters say drive the story.

Dialogue must move the story forward. The viewer needs to WANT to listen to hear what's being said, you have to make them get to that point by starting off on a good foot. When I write a novel I always start with dialogue. A character says something that gets attention, connected to an action. In the current book I'm working on I have a woman saying, "You do good work" to a man giving her a foot massage in an office environment.

Dialogue has to compound action. *"Ghostbusters"* (the original movie) pulls you in almost immediately based on what the characters are doing and saying. Memorable quotes are usually based on *well placed* dialogue, not just what's said, but the context and how it was said. "Nice shootin' tex..." is a memorable line from *"Ghostbusters"* said after one character blast everything with his proton pack but the ghost.

Another memorable line is from *"When Harry met Sally,"* when an older woman says, "I'll have what she's having," in reference to Sally (Meg Ryan) showing off her orgasm faking skills in a restaurant.

In the original *"Basic Instinct"* Detective Nick Curran (played by Michael Douglas) says, "Lets have a talk, man to man." This is a cliché and holds little weight unless you know he's saying it to Roxy (Leilani Sarelle) a dangerous woman who also happens to be lesbian and whose also involved with the deadly Catherine Tramell (Sharon Stone), who Curran is investigating and also attracted to. This scene ends with Roxy chasing him with a car which is quite funny actually after all the tough talk. I love that movie.

Have fun with dialogue, keep it fresh. Decide will your character be the person who talks like everyone else or the person that says what you (and others) would like to say, but don't. What makes people on screen cool is that many of them are not like us. Many say and do what we can only (or would only) imagine. The dialogue should make people want to continue to watch your story. You should find that point between being clever and honest.

CGI You hear this term a lot but it just means Computer Generated Image/ Imagery. The Hulk was a CGI, so are all the new animated movies like "Cars". The image is then created and composited into the shot. Usually it's not added in the script, but if you're shooting for yourself you can add a note.

Compositing is when one image is laid on top of another to achieve an effect. Normally a primary clip is shot against a specific color of blue or green material. That color is then taken out in the post process leaving that area invisible so the whatever was under the clip it is now seen as the background and appears to be part of the same image. This works for placing people in locations they really couldn't be in, adding explosions and just doing things you really couldn't do in real life. This is also done in Photoshop (see the poster creation tutorial).

Mechanical or **Practical Effects** are old school effects like knives or props that bleed, make-up effects, break-aways, blank guns, squib hits and anything not done on a computer or in-camera, is a Mechanical Effect.

```
              POLICE SERGEANT (o.s)
         Break it down.

Ted runs to the window and opens it.

CGI: Ted Flies off.
```

Ted flying could simply be a low angled shot from outside with a CGI of Ted flying being composited over it. Or mostly could simply be Ted standing against a blue or green screen or with a fan blowing on him then laid over the skyward shot and moved via your software's animation controls.

Note: If you are writing to sale a screenplay noting the effects is not done or proper screenwriting format. This is done in the shooting script for post purposes unless you're doing all the work then you may leave these notes to yourself.

PRODUCTION 101

Okay, it's now down to the wire. You got your equipment, but you need to get production started. What do you do next? This is how you proceed.

Production Documents

This is easily overlooked, but you should always have contracts whether you're doing a film, music video or a prank video.

Model Agreement: This is most important. You have the right to do almost whatever you want (that's legal and within reason) with their image in regard to them being in the film and your promotion of the movie. You need a good contract that states this.

Injury Release: Doing action, pranks or anything even remotely risky you will need this form. This is a form that cheerleaders, high school football players and others have to sign. It holds you harmless from actors who may get injured on set. The key is reasonable precaution has to be taken plus actors may refuse to do anything they deem dangerous.

Location Releases: These are needed to show that people have allowed you to shoot in their building, home, etc, especially if you've paid money for it. This is so they can't come back later and say they didn't allow it. Location releases may also hold you harmless in the case of damage, such as small scrapes and such, but will also make you responsible for big damage as no one will let you shoot in a location if you're really going to damage it and no one is left to pay for it.

Crew Releases: This often gets washed over. Most people don't even have crew releases. These are basically contracts stating under what circumstances the crew is working with you and if there is any pay or not and what their duties will be (even if they have multiple duties).

As a low budget filmmaker you probably won't need all of these, but I'll tell about the ones you should have. (The more you have the better it is for you).

Barter Agreements: If you do a service or help someone out because they're helping you out, put it in writing.

Contact Sheet: We talked about this before, a sheet of paper, preferably typed, with everyone's name and contact info on it. Mainly cell phone, home phone numbers and emails.

Call Sheets: These break down what's supposed to happen on that day. You should send these out to everyone participating that day, but many times you may not get the chance and things can change during shooting.

A call sheet normally contains the film's title, the date, the location information, props needed, who the what actors should be there that day, what they should be wearing (most times you will not be providing wardrobes unless it's something specific) and what time the actors will need to be on set. I usually have everyone there at once because sometimes you finish early and want to move onto the next thing and it gets confusing with actors moving in and out at differing times.

Shot Sheets: Have a list of all the shots you want to get done that day for the scene. Be realistic about your goals. You don't have to do these, but they do help. I normally know what I want so I forsake a shot list but during combat scenes they come in handy because you can easily forget to "match up" as I have done. In the scene where Makayla's character throws a balled up paper cup at me, there is no shot where I'm seen actually dodging it.

Organization:

Being organized is so important. This can make or break your film. On "Beast" we did a lot of run and gun style work. On *"Wages of Sin"* we had a lot more organization and control. I called people a week in advance to find out about locations. I put ads on Craigslist and offered a little money for specific types of places like the storefront (which had great horror film style basement that we didn't use).

First thing's first: At this point I'm assuming you've got your script done so now you have to pick a day to start production. I always choose some time in mid June.

Now start saving specific pages to send to actors. Each major character should have a segment of the script to read. These are called **Sides**. Save them as PDFs to send to those who need them.

Make up your flyers and set out your Craigslist ads. Your date should be about two months and a few days away. If you're shooting on July 15th, then start putting the word out May 1st so in June you'll have your casting call around the first of the month and your casting will be done by the middle of the month when you can start doing reads.

Eidetic Blocking

Blocking is when you run through the scene to get an idea where to place your camera and lights. It's a good chance you won't be able to get your locations constantly and get all your needed actors to said location to block so you'll need to remember how the location looks.

Since most of us don't have photographic memories go grab your camera and take photos of the location you'll be shooting at (if you haven't done it via scouting). Even if you know the location, because your mind probably isn't eidetic you should take photos or video of all the nooks and crannies.

Now you study those pictures to create and imagine how the scene will go down. We did this with Riti's character in the scene when she assassinates Richard Hokkaido. That scene had been thought out and planned so when time came I knew what the scene would look like even though I didn't know exactly what the room would look like, but I had the idea of a couch, a table, how she would enter, etc. That's how we made a classroom look like an office lounge. Even people who went to Columbia didn't know it was a classroom.

Everything worked out but, if I had it to do over I would've liked to knock the light out coming through the window because on televisions it doesn't look good. Many people still watch DVDs on their televisions (including me) versus digital downloads or even watching DVDs on their computers. On the computer the light coming through simply illuminates the scene more, but on a television it causes a nasty unprofessional looking glare.

Now at this point you need to be seriously thinking about how you plan to move the camera, how the scene will open and how it will close. Storyboard it if you want (there's tons of info online about how to story board). The more you visualize the scene the quicker you can pull it off.

Shopping

By this time you should already have any needed props in your possession. Go to the store to buy food the night before unless you have a car and will set out early, but if you go the night before it saves you from having to wake up much earlier than you already have to. (Unless your shoot is in the evening).

By this time:
1. Call sheets should have gone out if needed
2. Contact list should be complete
3. Special props obtained

4. All equipment is checked and ready
5. Extra batteries for camera and mic
6. All Model Releases should be signed
7. All Injury Releases should be signed
8. Actors should know where and when to meet and what to wear to the set
9. You should have a general idea of the blocking

Your production Binder Should Contain:

1. Call sheet for the day
2. Blank Call Sheets
3. Extra copies of the scenes to be shot that day
4. Extra Model Releases
5. Extra Injury Releases
6. Location releases
7. Barter agreements and IOUs
8. Shot sheet

Film Shoots

Run through the scene with your actors so everyone knows what to expect. Let them do a quick read through, then go without the script to see where any problem areas may be. Let them do some practice in the environment before you shoot. Decide your shot ratio (how many retakes you're willing to do based on budget and time).

Set up the lighting early. You and the crew need to arrive first. Blocking should be set for the first scene as the actors arrive and practice. Try to start at nine and end at five or before. Twelve-hour days are for shoots with money (or very patient actors and crew). Don't wear out your welcome with your people. Get your shot sheet out and get ready.

Vlogging

If you're vlogging a lot of the above may not apply, but Shoot the **B-roll** first. B-roll is defined as "supplemental or alternative footage intercut with the main shot." This can be used for cutaways, or to enhance your video's narrative such as showing drone footage or quick cuts of the area you're visiting or, if you know what you're going to talk about, get shots pertaining to that. Some people just do daily video journals with B-roll and voice over.

You should carry at least two cameras for a planned vlog, your A or main camera and a B cam which will do the B-roll so your footage doesn't get mixed up. Also your B cam is your back up so if something happens to your A cam, (batteries die, camera malfunctions, etc.) you won't completely lose out. I used to vlog on an old Sony NEX F3 with an Sj7 Star as B-cam, but currently I use the SJ7 Star to vlog and SJ6 as B-Cam, but I can have up to three cameras as I have quite a collection of Action Cameras.

Your least intrusive and easiest to use camera, (usually your compact, action cam or phone), is your "grab and go" camera, which is one you take everywhere with you. It should always have an SD card and battery.

After shooting the B-roll shoot your main stuff. Sometimes just shooting B-roll will give you more inspiration for your vlog, especially if you're light on ideas.

If you're just shooting a vlog where the camera is on you all the time and you're just talking into it, this may not be as important.

Matching up

In filmmaking, matching up is when you take the same shot from a different angle to allow seamless movement to the next cut. This means you can show a person block a punch, then break the 180° and shoot this again. In editing you can do a "cut on the action," so as the attacker moves to punch, cut to the other angle as it gets blocked then cut back. (This is another way you can shoot from the opposite side of the 180° line).

In dialogue scenes matching is used to transition from cut to cut. In shooting dialogue, get the establishing shot out of the way first, then before you do any other shots, you need to get these shots.

1. A medium side view of the whole conversation (this is called a two shot)
2. An over the shoulder shot of the first person speaking
3. An over the shoulder shot of the other person speaking
4. A medium close up (front view) of each actor doing their lines
5. Get a close up of each actor from the front doing the lines.

I'm assuming you have only 1 camera for this shoot and otherwise you can shoot scenes from multiple angles at one time.

Over the shoulder shot. To match this shot You'd do the same angle from behind the Woman with him on the right and her on the left.

These five things are a must. This is all "matched". You have an over the shoulder for each person, a close up and the two shot. If push comes to shove you can still do a full dialogue scene if you have these five kinds of shots. Any other trick shots or cool things you want to do should be shot after this stuff is done.

Catching Action

Actions such a running or even moving along with a person walking, are caught by either dollying with the subject or moving with the camera while holding it on some kind of a stabilizer. Most low budget filmmakers turn on the image stabilization and simply walk or run with the camera. This can work, but sometimes it simply doesn't and "shaky cam" is played out.

I ran around in a circle shooting the last fight scene in *"The Fourth Beast"* film and many people say it's the best shot in the film. *"Wages of Sin"* had a sideways tilt that people thought was pretty slick. We were able to get more technical because we weren't being rushed out of locations. We got to do multiple lighting set ups and practice some shots. The planning paid off.

The shot of Riti walking to meet Jin's character (the "butt shot" as it's become known around here) was done on a "Truck Dolly" which is what is used to cart huge boxes and such around in grocery stores. Columbia has a bunch of them and we got one for film. I got caught up in using the truck dolly — it was so "professional" — the best takes were the ones we shot on our basic spreader dolly, go figure.

The camera should always be moving. Static shots are okay for conversations and even then there should be cuts. People have short attention spans now days so long conversations need to keep a certain pace.

I'm into dialogue and story. Action with no story is crap. "The Transporter" 1 and 2 had good stories and interesting characters, 3 was okay. You liked the Transporter and wanted to see him get the bad guys even though he wasn't that far off from being a badguy himself. Another good one is "Kiss of the Dragon" with Jet Li. This was one of the inspirations for *Wages of Sin*.

Booming

The key to booming is keep the mic still and tape the cord to the side of the boom pole. Indie boom poles are usually painter's rods with microphones screwed on them. (Painter's use collapsible poles use for painting ceilings). There are screw on microphone holders specifically made to go on to these poles to turn them into makeshift boom poles. Painter's poles are light and hollow, actual boom poles are a little heavier.

Either way if the wire strikes against the pole you will hear it, if someone is constantly moving their hand around the pole you will hear it. This is true for any boom set up. A "fuzzy" is used to cut down on wind on outside shoots.

So before you shoot: 1. First tape the mic cord to the poles with duct or electrical tape so only part that moves is the part trailing at the end of the pole. 2. Grip the boom firmly and do not let it move around in one's hand or it will be heard. Hold the boom high with the mic pointed between the two people speaking (assuming the mic is a cardioid). Also, as stated before you can screw a Zoom H1 on to a monopod or light stand and not have to worry about the wire.

The Three Kinds of Microphones:

Uni-Directional which hears sound from one direction and that's whatever direction it's pointing at.

Cardioid captures sound in a heart shaped pattern.

Omni-Directional which captures sound from all around. Your camera's onboard mic is usually omni-directional.

You want to use a **cardioid** or uni-directional mic. The uni-directional has to be turned toward each person who speaks. The sound is very good, but the cardioid is more practical. Frankly, for certain scenes you can put a cardioid on a telescoping microphone stand and raise it over and between the actors, put it on the base and it will pick up perfect sound without worrying about human error (unless someone forgets to turn it on).

Earphones are important also. No, you can't use the ones you use with your iPod or laptop, you should get a pair of good ones if possible, the ones that have thick padding covering the ears and cost about $40 — $100. It's important for you to hear how the sound is coming in through the mic. You will pick up hums and static from electrical equipment, bumps from upstairs and next-door neighbors and everything else.

You may have to unplug things close to the mic because they may make a buzz. All of this is hard to work with in post and many times impossible to work with without doing ADR. You don't want to have to do ADR; you want clean sound from jump. You'll have enough sound work to do as it is. Without good earphones you may miss unwanted sound coming in to the mic.

Presence is the sound you hear when there is no sound. That means no one is walking, talking or doing anything. Everyone is silent. This is called room presence. You should get everyone quiet record thirty to sixty-seconds of it to lay under scenes, especially if ADR is involved.

Directing

Respect your actors, but don't be afraid to say do it over or show them the way you want it to be done or even the inflection. Sometimes actors have it in their head how the scene should be done and you have to keep telling or showing them what you want until they get it right.

As I mentioned before, I used to believe, "Actors acted" therefore I should be minimally invasive with my approach to directing. The reality is this doesn't work for everyone. There's a big difference in the acting quality between "Wages" and "Fourth" and it's noticeable. I had more time to spend with actors and tell them what was needed in "Wages" plus we got to do read-throughs on some of the more dramatic scenes.

Also you need to be descriptive with an actor. If you say, "I want you to act scared then run," that's a big difference than saying, "I want you to draw back in shock, take a few steps back, look around for away out and run toward the back stairs."

Don't be afraid to direct while shooting the scene. If there is no dialogue you can tell the actor what to do as they're acting. Remember you can cut your voice out of the scene and add presence, (you did record presence right?) and/or music.

Designing Your World

What do Michael Mann and I have in common? Outside of our savvy and our lush lifestyles? We both like to shoot outside night shots in video. (The savvy and lush lifestyle part is generally untrue, that's just him). Actually since it's all video now days, I should say we like to shoot night scenes with the "video look" versus the "film look".

But when video is put on film it too becomes filmic so it loses what I believe we're both going for and that is the look of the television show "Cops". I wanted to do this in *"Wages of Sin"* but didn't fearing that the distributors wouldn't like it. This was a mistake, because I ended up doing self-distribution anyway. Next time I'll get the look I want.

My thought was, "All the low budget stuff is shot in 24p DV now days so if I shot night scenes in 60i (60 interlaced frames per second, which is the standard rate of American television) they wouldn't 'get it'. Distributors make money not art." (Not that I was specifically making "art," but I did play around with some looks and try some cool things).

You have to design your world based on your vision. Consider how a room should look or what colors your actors should wear. How did you see it in your head? My world was based on the contrast between light and dark. Obviously the Cop = the light, versus the underworld = the darkness, so the cop was the light in the darkness.

We shot on the corner of Clark and Division, which is a party street. It's all lit up, with clubs and lights everywhere, but it's somewhat grimy looking. Add in a few women in mini skirts and you have an instant red-light district. (Even though we don't at this time officially have red-light districts in Chicago there are locations we somewhat consider RLDs).

I love the scene as it is but I want to go back and capture it in 1080i HD video. I also want to shoot a whole horror film at 1080i with a 35mm adapter attached. (I know, after so much work to get video to look like film).

Set Design for Microbudget Projects

Microbudget filmmakers are known for messing this up. I myself have been a victim of bad set design (or having no design at all). **Set design** is basically designing the look of your set.

When you're doing set design you have to consider *Mise en scène* a fancy French word that means "to put on stage".

This is all about the information the single shot conveys based on what's shown or happening in the scene. There's a difference between having a character enter a bathroom and having them enter a dingy, dank, grime-ridden bathroom. Subconsciously a lot of information is being given. The place is filthy, hasn't been cleaned in a long time and is well traveled possibly by dingy, dank, grime-ridden people. These type of places are normally found in horror films. This should make the character take pause and the actions that character takes in even this situation helps define them, their location and may help foreshadow upcoming events.

The grime on the walls and sink are not left there naturally (that's gross), it's set design. Grime can be made from mixing planter's dirt with flour and water then spread over the toilet, sink and walls (if the walls have tile on them). The mixture is spread thin, then washed off once the scene is shot.

Set design is about information and imagery as shown in the example above. Things match up (or not) to put forth mental notes that tell the story, such as having a man dressed in a tailored suit walking around in a poorly lit, unkempt hallway of a slum apartment building. This doesn't fit so we immediately want to know why this person is there and what's going to happen to them.

Most modern apartment interiors (at least here in the city) are basic white walled drudgery. A painting or paintings are normally hung to get rid of this effect. The paintings should convey something about the apartment owner as well as the style of the apartment. (Make sure you have copyright permission and give credit for the painting if needed).

There are questions that should be asked when doing set design. Is the person, rich, middle class or poor. Do they have a computer or video game system? Do they have a landline phone or only use a cell phone? What kind of clothes are in their closet. What's the purpose of the scene? What kind of environment does the scene take place in? You get the point.

There's two good ways to get stuff for set design, the number one way (aside from bringing stuff from home) is Goodwill or some other place that sells used stuff for cheap. You'd be surprised at what you can get for cheap.

Another way is Craigslist. Again good ol' Craig's. People give away stuff on Craigslist all the time, totally free. The only thing is you have to come pick it up. It may or may not be there when you go for it.

Stock Footage

When you want to get helicopter footage, blow up a building, or do anything you can't afford, take a look at stock footage. This is video footage of various things sold to filmmakers and news studios.

Say you want to do a car chase and have a car fall over a cliff. There may be stock footage of a car going over a cliff, so now you have to match the car in the scene with the car going over the cliff then cut the stock footage into the scene in a way that it looks believable.

Some big companies like Sony sale clips from their films for this purpose. You probably can't afford these. iStockphoto.com sales stock SD and HD video too and at reasonable prices. So if you have an account with them it's pretty sweet. This is one of the best places to get your stock art, photos or video from and (one of the cheapest for video).

According to one of their press releases they have *"Over 90,000 royalty-free video clips available for as little as $10 each and offer "the flexibility of royalty-free licensing along with the quality from some of the world's best artists."* Like their photo collection, their video stock can help give you a pro look for cheap.

Pixabay is a donation based stock photo company. They don't have as many photos, but the one's they have are great, and also free, even for commercial use. They do ask for a voluntary donation to the photographer which is only fair. I used this site for the cover and some of the interior photos.

Beg and Borrow and Shop
As an indie filmmaker you're going to come up against the problem we all face: "how to get stuff".

Costumes
Watch any big or even grade-B Hollywood movie and notice what the actors are wearing. Only certain types of characters wear jeans and a T-shirt and many times those have some kind of writing or something on them that matches the character's disposition. The movie *"The Last Action Hero"* takes a comical look at this, the idea was, in the "Action Movie" world everyone was beautiful all the time, but outside of that world people simply were not. The movie was actually a lot of fun and very effective at showing the difference.

To enhance clothing pick up any fashion magazine. You'll need a men's and women's magazine, get one that's "classy"and one that's "urban". Look at all the expensive fashions and copy them. Tell your actors to wear something similar, but stay away from stripes and crazy patterns if you can. Believe it or not, that adds production value. You can tell each actor to wear specific things that most people have, but when put together with something specific it will match up to what's in the magazines, but at a fraction of the cost. A lot of our actors wore suits. In "Wages" our actresses wore various outfits based on the scenes they were in and the matching scarves the badguys wore were actually one of the actors' idea, in fact he brought them.

In Chicago we have a store called Ragstock, they resale vintage clothes at a low price and sale new clothes at a decent price as well. Last time I was there they had full tuxedos for about $31 (they sold the pants for $10, shirts for $6 and the jackets for $10 and the ties for $5 plus tax). I got a cool leather coat for $28. There's also theft stores and The Salvation Army, which is a great cause and can be totally raided for both clothes and props. $50 — $100 can get you all kinds of stuff there.

Only buy special clothes for actors, that includes special articles of clothing or expendables, (clothes that may get "bloody", dirty or torn). Otherwise let them wear their own clothes. We worked with Riti, who was a former Ms. India and had her own designer so she always looked awesome. CiCi had many different dresses, skirts and pants. We shot at her house one day so she had easy access to everything and looked totally hot in all her scenes.

Say you have a pair of shoes you want your actress to wear. Ask why do you want her to wear those shoes and what do they mean to the story? Then you want to see if the actress has similar shoes. If so, you just saved yourself $50 — $100 as women's shoes are unreasonably expensive. If not, then the next step is looking for the free stuff on Craigslist and shopping eBay, but before that check with the local Salvation Army. And online shoe stores that sell cheaper or (usually overstock), shoes.

The example above is generally how you buy things for microbudget films. And you have to remember your business plan. Ask, "Who do I know?" My mother can sew (and so can I a little bit). If you want a character to wear a miniskirt and you have a stretchy piece of material, fold it over and sew it together at the side, then pull the actress' top over the waistline of the skirt. Save $9 — $20. We did this in "The Fourth Beast" for a character and it worked fine. In fact we had to keep an eye on the actress because so many dudes were checking her out. You should learn to sew as it can come in handy for quick accessories and costumes.

Vampire teeth can be found for cheap on eBay. Buy the cheesy plastic kind for the vampires in the background and the kind that stick on the canines for all your star vampires, this is a B-movie trick.

Props
We talked about getting props before and using what you know you can get, but you may also have to learn how to build these. Learn to use your imagination. A break-away table can be made with left over wood from Home Depot or Balsa wood and a can of stain. Buy a 4 x 5 foot board about a third to half of an inch thick.

Cut the board in the middle so that it looks like it's broke, but leave it slightly connected so it will stand. (If you're not an adult you should have adult supervision when using tools). Cut one of the legs in the middle. Nail the flat piece onto the four equal size legs, line the cut leg up. Paint or stain it. When the paint dries throw a table cloth over it (or not). Set some soft props on it, like papers, napkins, empty soda cans and such (so it won't look like it's just their to get smashed) and when your stunt guy falls or is thrown through it, it should fall apart easily.

Wooden bow staffs cost a lot of money, but you can get a five foot wooden dowel, (a half inch to an inch in diameter) from most hardware stores for about six bucks. Round off the ends with a sander (or don't, it's up to you). and if you want, you can also run it slowly across an open fire to let it burn part of the wood to char it to give it a professional look. Then stain it and spray enamel on it for a shine. This looks great for those close ups. The stain and enamel will be used again in your other builds.

Warning: *Take precautions when staining or painting (or burning). You want to be in a well ventilated area, and wearing protective ventilation mask is also a great idea.*

Need to make that drug transaction look real? Powdered sugar or baking soda will do the trick. You can buy fake money online or from novelty shops. You can also get it printed, but you'll need a letter stating why you're doing it, that you won't use it to counterfeit (you may want to get this letter notarized) and you will have to disfigure your money by taking the name of the Treasurer and the Secretary of the Treasury off and making other alterations so people can tell it's not real. But on screen, when it's in a roll, bundle or strapped together in a brick, it won't be noticeable that it's not real.

Found Props
Don't be so quick to throw things away. Get a big trunk to save things in. Save wine and champagne bottles (and the cork), and cans with lids. Wash them out and use them later in background. Champagne bottles can be filled with the cheap cream soda you buy at the discount grocery store to make it look like champagne again. Cream soda will also burst out when shaken and the cork is popped and red or white sparkling grape juice makes great wine, sparkling grape juice makes great champagne.

Also women are key. When finding props, seek out your female friends. A lot of ladies have tons of stuff they don't need, but you do. Start with your mom, sisters, girlfriend or wife and their friends and move on. They have clothes, make up and trinkets they'll never use again, but simply haven't thrown it away. (They also have shoes they'll never wear).

Hit up friends. Actor and producer Jon Ross gave me a freaking wheel chair. I haven't used it yet, but if I ever need a wheelchair prop or a quick dolly, I have one. (People do just give you stuff sometimes).

People who're moving have tons of stuff they don't want or need. Many times they'll give it to you for free. If you need to break up a bunch of stuff buy all those cheap vases from the Salvation Army, Goodwill or a thrift store and buy a cheap paint ball gun. Use dust hits (you can find companies that offer paintballs filled with dust). Load up the paint gun and shoot brick walls and things that will fall or break easily, then cut to the person cowering, jumping and/or crawling around as if being shot at.

You can also put a bunch of plastic items in a bag and break them up with a bat, then use the small pieces to scoop up and throw at the actor to replicate debris during those medium close ups. The actor covers their face with their arms and continues to move as if being shot at.

Warning: *Be sure to do good clean up after this. You want to sweep, mop, vacuum and if possible, do not use glass for any of this.*

Notice of Upcoming Film Shoot

One thing you should do, especially when shooting an action film, is give notice. A notice is basically an 8.5 x 11 or 8 x 14 page that has a header in big black letters that says: *"NOTICE: FILM SHOOT"* with the date listed this will tell people you will be shooting in that area on that date. The beauty of this is it notifies the people in that area so they won't freak if they see anything weird happening and it also advertises your film and may even alert the media.

After your header there should be a breakdown:
"On (date listed in header) we will be shooting our film (name of production). This film will include scenes of martial arts, stunts, action and vampires (or whatever oddities your film may have)." This is to let people know what will be happening this day. *"We will be shooting in the area of (list places you will be shooting that may be nearby) from (list the time you will start to time you will finish)."*

If you have celebrities or a celebrity, (even B-list celebrities) write:
"We are shooting the (name celebrity) film (name movie). This film will include scenes of martial arts, stunts and action. We will be shooting in the area of (list places you will be shooting that may be nearby) from (list time you will start to time you will finish)."

If the celebrity is not one of the main stars you can write:
We are shooting the film (name film) with (name celebrity)....

The rest should read: "This project will not interfere with the day to day workings of your businesses or home, but we wanted to inform you as to what would be happening on this day so that if you were to run across our production you will know what is happening."

"Thank you for your time. For more information please visit us on the web at (list website). If you would like to help out please let us know as we still need (list things you may need or want for the film if you would like people to help out)."

Once your flyers are made then you have the tedious task of walking around taping them to the windows of business establishments (preferably after they're closed) and apartment building doors. If you are shooting inside an apartment building no notice is needed, unless there will be loud noise or something that may disturb the residents, but normally if you're shooting inside of an apartment there should be no problem. If you will be in the halls you may need to provide notice to the building and the renter may need to provide notice to their landlord.

Notice of Film in Progress

The next notice you will need to give is the notice of a shoot in progress when in public places, and it goes a little something like this:

"Please note that (production company) is in the progress of shooting the independent (add film genre, action, comedy, romance, horror) film (add name of the film) in this location. By entering this location, you give your consent to be videotaped, photographed and/or recorded.

You grant the producer and their assignees and all in association with the production the unrestricted right of use of the images and recordings of your image, likeness and/or voice, to create, exhibit and distribute by any means they chose without compensation.

You hereby release the producer, their assignees and all in association with the production of any and all claims or causes of legal action without limitations including libel, defamation, invasion of privacy or right of publicity."

This should also be on an 8.5 x 11 or 8.5 x 14 sheet of paper in bold black letters in all caps so people can see it. This notice should be on the doors and at various places where people will have to pass.

View the Dailies

Thanks to modern technology, this can done between sit up and breakdowns, but it's better to do after all the shooting is done for the day because you don't want to accidentally record over anything. If you're using tape, you rewind the tapes all the way back and watch everything you shot.

Most of today's cameras use cards or internal drive systems so you recall or click on each scene and watch it from your camera or laptop. You can easily go through an eight-hour day, shoot only two hours of footage and from that only use about four to ten minutes. If you get ten good minutes that was a great day.

Learn The Process

This not a filmmaking book, but if you really want to learn how to shoot and edit, there's so many Youtube videos out here that show you how to do it. While I'm a huge fan of books I love seeing how it's done. Once you learn the process you will be able to repeat it over and over again and get better and better at it.

EDITING AND POST

Now you're ready to edit the day's work. Some people have a laptop on set and they can simply off load the footage from the card to a harddrive and start editing right there. This means another crew member, (or yourself) may have to work on the computer between set up.

Editing

You will generally be presented with a long space where you will place clips from a storage bin and with a razor blade tool you will cut the clips or pick "in" and "out" points where you want them to start or stop. There will be other ways to do this in the program too that will be more precise called trimming. Also, learn to use timecode. Almost every major editing program has *timecode*: a group of numbers the computer uses to recognize the frames in a video clip. Put these numbers in the order you want your shots to fall and the computer will do the rest.

Start picking out your clips and putting everything together. Don't wait until you have all the footage, start the process ASAP. As you shoot and get more clips arrange them in the order they belong. This is what will become your rough. You will go in and trim more carefully to make the film look cleaner and more professional.

When you cut the film the sound will come with it. In most professional NLEs you can separate the sound and the video if need be.

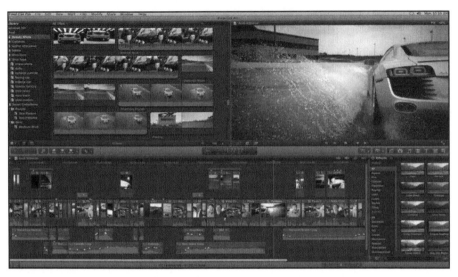

The all new interface for Final Cut Pro X. Check out the magnetic timeline and built in effects.

You will also find places where the lighting is off from one shot to another. You will need to color correct this. Various programs have their own ways of doing it. Apple used to have a separate program called "Color" but it now has been seemingly merged with Final Cut Pro X.

Set up your effects shots to be imported into your compositing program if you're using one. A program called Automatic Duck can make this a one step process on Final Cut Pro 5 - 7 and Apple Motion is integrated with Final Cut Pro X but sold separately and After Effects, of course, is integrated with Premiere Pro, but also sold separately unless you buy a bundle. Most of the Adobe Programs can be subscribed to now and used from the cloud.

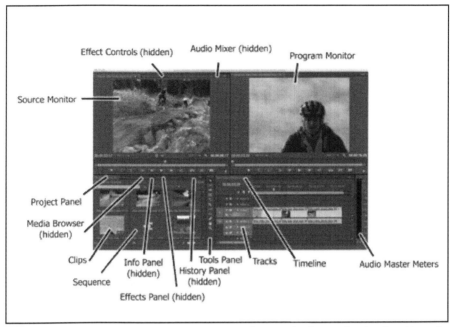

Premiere's Pro's interface: Most editing programs have a clip bin and a timeline. You take clips from the bin and drag them to the timeline simple.

As for the actual editing I can't begin to teach you everything you need to know, there's tons of books and Youtube vids on it. It's really something you will have to learn on your own. Timing is a key element, especially if you're doing a micro-budget movie. Knowing when to "cut away" or "cut to" something is an essential skill. Sometimes you'll get an actor who does a really good scene, but messes up that last part, and you don't want to ditch the whole scene so you'd cut to a reaction shot. Or in a shoot out you have to cut very quickly as to create the chaos of a gun battle especially since you can't shoot things up like in the big movies until you've dressed the set properly, then you have to take quick shots of the damage.

Post Sound

Sound is more difficult than the rest. Sound has to be level, which means you don't want people to have to turn their television up and down to hear what's being said. This starts in production. Sound needs to come in clean that way all you need to do is either turn it up or down.

You should have your camera connected to a television or NTSC monitor via the RCA jacks (most cameras have some form of output from camera to television) and headphone. If your settings are correct you should be able to see the video on the television screen once you scroll through it. (Unless it's HD and your set is SD).

You should also be able to get a good idea how your sound will come out for the average viewer. Our sound was horrible on parts of *"The Fourth Beast"*. It turns out there was an internal break in the microphone cord, so while I was getting sound in the headphones it was second channel, which was being recorded through the camera mic. This sound was very different from the shotgun mic's audio and it wasn't as good. There was nothing I could really do about it. In "Wages" we had a new cord and had a boom guy on every shoot and we don't use the on camera mic at all, so we know whether sound is in or not.

Now that you have all your major sound together you need effects. You will find that your karate and great gunfights look very silly with no sound effects. It's true if you take away sound, action movies can look really stupid.

Go to Sounddogs.com for a bunch of free sound effects. Better yet if you can afford Videocopilot's "Designer Sound Effects" get it. It will be a big help but Sounddogs is very good and very reasonable (it's free), besides DSF doesn't have any practical effects most of their stuff is for commercials, but you'll need that too and some of the impact sounds are awesome.

Final Cut Pro X and iMovie comes with a bunch of effects.

Using Music on Youtube

This is where tons of problems start. Let's be clear about something right off the bat, Smashing Pumpkin's *"Doomsday Clock"* and DMX's *"X Gonna Give it to 'Em"* are both awesome action songs, and back in the day if you use them there was a very good chance you'd get sued for copyright infringement. But under the Youtube model you get the hated Content ID match which can lead to the dreaded copyright strike.

Content ID Matches

This means content in your video has matched someone else's copy written material. This usually happens with music, but can happen with video. This means a company or group has to look at your video and see if the match is accurate and if so they decide whether to issue a take down notice or have a link added to your video telling people where to get the music used.

Copyright Strikes

A copyright strike is many times confused with an ID Match and they are different. A copyright strike means your content can be stricken from Youtube. Just recently I had to file several copyright complaints, because a person had not only re-uploaded my film "Epitaph: Bread and Salt," but had monetized it. I contacted this person and they told me I had to prove it was my film. (Keep in mind he knew it wasn't his). Obviously he didn't know how copyright worked. Not only would he not take it down, he would upload again to several different accounts all which were removed by Youtube. Also keep in mind my film was on my company's Youtube channel.

But not only does a copyright strike endanger your project, you can be locked out of monetization for up to six months and even lose your account so you want to do your due diligence to make sure all your content is indeed your own.

Content ID Match Scams

If you're on a modern Mac (think 2012 and up), you have probably GarageBand; if you're on a PC you probably have the alternative (Fruity Loops). You bought a cheap MIDI keyboard from eBay and now you're ready to make that killer sound track. These programs come with music loops that are free to use, the only thing you can't do it sell or copyright the loops themselves. But wait...

One of the issues with Youtube is, it opens the doors for scammers. Some of these scammers have gone so far as to copyright Apple and other loops as well as other people's royalty and public domain content. These people open copyright claims on random Youtubers. If you allow it they can make money from your hard work, but if you fight, they may have the ability to have your movie or episode stricken from Youtube via false copyright claim. Youtube has done a lot better recently with stopping false DCMA claims and takedowns, but people can still abuse it.

Sometimes the ID match is a mistake, matching a loop in your music with a song that uses the same loop. The ID system is automated and has very little oversight. Youtube says a DCMA claim has to be filled, to have you some videos removed, but that doesn't seem to be the case. It works when someone uploads your stuff to their page, but not so much so when you're being hit with the strike and all your stuff is your own. While these companies do have a process to remedy these situations many people find them either intimidating or fruitless. But either way, it's safer to make your own music for your projects. (Although recently I find just emailing some of these companies will solve the problem).

Where to get Free Music

Aside from the free music Youtube offers in the Creator Studio (click on the "Create" link) companies like No Copyright Sounds (NCS) or No Copyright Tracks (NCT) and others offer copyright free music for your use, as long as you credit the creators in your credits and add their links in you description.

A lot of the music from these channels are pretty good and there's usually a lot to choose from.

Output for Viewing

So after all of that you are done with your film. Now what? In "Action Filmmaking" I broke down how you output for DVD. But now, we're talking Youtube and streaming video. So you're going to output your video.

If you're on a Mac using Final Cut Pro X, you have a "Share" button, which will give you several options. And as you can see one of those options is "Youtube", but that option is only good for videos that are fifteen minutes or shorter. But if you are a Youtube partner you probably have an account enabled to upload much longer videos.

So what to do? First decide if you want to a 1080p project or a 720p project. 1080p is the standard, but Youtube is capable of 1080p, 2k and 4K streaming if your internet is fast enough and your computer and its graphics card are powerful enough to stream it.

Choose your **In Point** (the beginning) and the **Out Point** (the end of your project). Then click the "Share" button or go to the drop down under the "File" menu.

The default is "Master File". This means saving the file to a computer or external harddrive. If you save it as an "Apple Device" file it will also save to the computer in either a .MOV or .M4V (The H.264 codec) format, both work on Youtube.

On a PC, there's many various programs, but for the most part this is what you're going to do. Choose your In and Out Points and go to "Save" or "Export" depending on program. There should be a list of options. The options you will want are ".MP4" or ".MOV". You can also upload a WMV file, but MP4 or MOV are generally better options.

After you output your file, view it to make sure it plays right. Once all is good, you simply go to Youtube and upload then click the various options you want for your upload and you're done. The time it will take to upload will vary based on your internet speed.

SELF PROMOTION

Cutting the Youtube Trailer

Back in the day straight to video films were indeed sold on the poster and a trailer or mock trailer. Companies would get pre-sales and then make the movie. And back in Action Filmmaking I stated that wasn't the way business was done anymore, well surprise. You need to get a trailer fast to get listed on IMDB. That and the poster stands are your primary marketing pieces.

The trailer is basically some of your best scenes, cut over dialogue and dramatic music that tell the story. By the end of this people should have a general idea what the movie is about and be able to make a decision to see the film or not. You want them to decide to see it.

Now you have to jump into this and as soon as you have those great scenes you need to have a trailer. And you should make about three, your original teaser (about thirty-seconds), a new one with more info (also thirty seconds) and a longer one that last about sixty to ninety-seconds.

I cut many times, moving scenes, dialogue and music then clipping and trimming. You want to tell a lot of info at one time, (The Transporter 3 trailer does this well) until you get it to look as close to a professional trailer as possible.

Now this where it gets scary, you've spent your money, so where and how will you sale your movie? First burn a copy to DVD, download a copyright form from the US government copyright office at www.copyright.gov fill it out and send it in with your DVD and the proper payment. While this isn't a necessity under the new copyright law it's an added layer of protection and in America, needed to file a lawsuit.

Announce your Film to the World

Blogging is a great way of getting the word out, the only problem is you have to promote your blog. DVXUser already has a fan base and it's getting bigger and bigger. People will see your work and follow your blog.

Before I even started my film "Epitaph: Bread and Salt" I announced the plans on DVXuser.com, which is a popular hubsite for indie filmmakers. Originally it was a gathering place for owners of the DVX100, the first prosumer camcorder that could record 24 progressive frames a second (the same rate as film) for under $4000. This was eventually replaced by the HD capable HCM150.

The site has a "User Films" section for members actively making films. People can ask questions and give advice as they watch your film progress. It's a big deal to many indie filmmakers especially students.

To make waves there you have to be working on an exciting project that's going somewhere. There's a lot of good work there so just showing your "trailer" is no longer good enough.

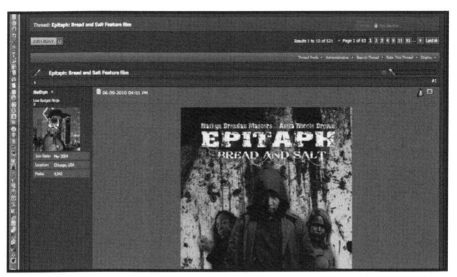

DVXUser's "User Films" section has a simple interface that almost anyone can use. This is the first page of our old production blog.

This is the first step in establishing a web presence for the film. And don't forget to make a Facebook Page for it and to submit your press releases to the genre sites. Just a few years ago I would've said you have to get into the trades, but today, the genre sites are where it's at, action, horror and indie cinema in general all have genre sites and it's up to you to find them. For me "Film Combat Syndicate", "Far East Films" and "Brutal As Hell" have all been helpful. I also use an inexpensive press release service.

Facebook, Twitter and other social networking sites are great ways to contact and connect with people like yourself who're into what you're into. There are social networking sites for filmmakers like Stage32.

Your website should pull everything together. Different service providers have different rules, but mainly you will buy a certain domain name then a certain amount of server space from a company such as Earthlink, Powweb or GoDaddy. You would have to pay every year for this space. Now days all you have to do is buy your domain name, and then point it to the location you want it to go which can be your blog, Youtube channel or a Facebook "Like" page. You can even use a free service like Wix and they will give you the space for free, but will place a small logo on your page. Wix is especially good for people who don't know how to build websites, but want a certain amount of creative control over their page.

Even though you're distributing though Youtube, you still will want to have copies to sell. Get an account with **Kunaki**. This is the quickest way to get a professional copy of your DVD. They have templates and everything you will need for packaging. Get your Photoshop person to do a cover and a face for the DVD or just use the original art if it's good enough. Do not use any copyrighted material.

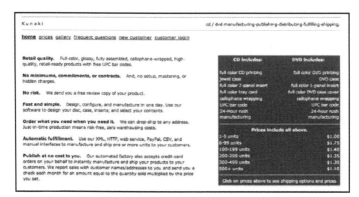

Once you get your proof back, look it over. Does it really look professional? Match it up to what's in the video store. You want to do what they do and if possible do it better. You don't have to match their style, but your micro-budget film doesn't have to have a micro-budget feel, your packaging quality should be on par with theirs.

Advertise your Film

Because your film is online you have a big advantage, a lot of free and cheap advertising options. Your first option of course is Facebook. They have a whole set–up for people looking to sell products. The advertising is cheap and click based.

Online press releases should always have a link to your Youtube page as should your website and business cards. If you have a "linkedIn", "Meet Me" or any social networking page you should be telling people about the project. Use a service like IFTTT.com (IF That Then This) which will allow you to post in one place and it will simultaneously post to your other social networks and even "Blogger" and "Wordpress" blogs. Use Buffer to post from Facebook to "LinkedIn" and "Google Plus". You can even use Youtube to advertise. Go to Youtube https://www.youtube.com/yt/advertise and go from there. This is also click based like Google's Adwords.

Descriptive Links Versus Click Bait

An honest descriptive link draws people who're interested in what you offer. Click Bait, shows a graphic and a suggestive title, but is never what it says and typically gets down-voted.

For our film "Epitaph: Bread and Salt" we titled it "Epitaph: Bread and Salt (2013) Full Movie Action / Martial Arts / Horror USA". You have the title of the film, the year it was released and the kind of film it is and the country of origin. For a music video you'd put the artist name, a dash, then the name of the video and then "(Official)" behind it. While "Official" is overused on Youtube, you should still use it.

Youtube Video Thumbnail

As a Partner you will have the choice to make your own thumbnail. The thumbnail pops up with the description of your video. Youtube offers a breakdown of how to set your thumbnail up. The Visual guidelines are as follows:

- Clear, in-focus, hi-resolution (640px x 360px min., 16:9 aspect ratio)

- Bright, high-contrast

- Close-ups of faces

- Visually compelling imagery

- Well-framed, good composition

- Foreground stands out from background

- Looks great at both small and large sizes

- Accurately represents the content

General Guidelines

- When shooting a video, take shots that will make great thumbnails

- Always upload custom thumbnails with the video file

- Design thumbnails that reinforce your videos' <u>titles</u> - make sure that together they tell a cohesive story

- Make sure the thumbnail is not overly sexually provocative (Which on Youtube you know is a toss up).

APPENDIX

For more Action Filmmaking Go To:

www.timecodemechanics.com

For Immediate Release

Masters Second Actioner Contemplates The "Wages of Sin"

CHICAGO, IL – TimeCode Mechanics frontman Nathyn Brendan Masters will reunite with indie producer John H. Rogers III to go into production on his second feature "Wages of Sin", formerly titled "Hit or Miss". Masters calls the film a "relentless low budget *ass kicker* with enough two fisted action to satisfy action lovers here and abroad."

"Wages" is the story of a sting operation gone array and a botched assassination attempt that leaves Johnny "Trigger", AKA deep cover officer Nathan Matthews framed for aiding and abetting in the murder of undercover officers, Tarantino and Rodriguez. Matthews befriends Teresa, a hooker who wants out of the street life. As luck would have it she's got the goods on Nathan's previous mark, up and coming drug kingpin Eric Constantine. Matthews must find the dirty cops, protect Teresa and evade goons, hit teams and an infamous assassin called "Mona Lisa", whose been hired by Constantine to kill them both.

The actors include, some of the usual TimeCode Mechanics suspects, such as Michael MacRae, Glenn Dhont and martial artist Shawn Bernal. Mix three beautiful new faces, CiCi Foster, Felicia Danisor and former Ms. India Riti Madugula into the fray and you've got all the right ingredients. Danisor helms the role of Jazz, a street savvy prostitute who's grown to love the illicit street life. Foster plays Teresa, a reluctant newcomer to the streets who wants out and Madugula takes on the role of killer for hire Mona Lisa.

To add realism the crew plans to shoot in some of Chicago's seedier neighborhoods. "I actually wanted to shoot this in a sort of Michael Mann style. I knew what he was getting at shooting the night scenes in HD. The video look adds a certain type of beauty to the night but also a certain type of grit.

For more information contact R. Mavers at: info@timecodemechanics.com
Contact Number # 312-555-5555
General Website: http://www.timecodemechanics.com

SAMPLE MODEL/ACTOR RELEASE

In consideration of my engagement as an actor/actress, upon the terms herewith stated, I hereby give to "Big J Productions", Bobby J. Filmmaker, his heirs, companies, legal representatives and assigns, those for whom photographer's name goes here is acting, and those acting with his authority and permission:

a)   The unrestricted right and permission to copyright and use, re-use, publish, and republish photographic portraits, images or motion pictures of me or in which I may be included intact or in part, composite or distorted in character or form, without restriction as to changes or transformations in conjunction with my own or a fictitious name, or reproduction hereof in color or otherwise, made through any and all media now or hereafter known for illustration, art, promotion, advertising, trade, or any other purpose whatsoever.

b)   I also permit the use of any printed or video material in connection therewith.

c)   I hereby relinquish any right that I may have to examine or approve the completed product or products or the advertising copy or printed matter that may be used in conjunction therewith or the use to which it may be applied.

d)   I hereby release, discharge and agree to save harmless [photographer], his/her heirs, legal representatives or assigns, and all persons functioning under his/her permission or authority, or those for whom he/she is functioning, from any liability by virtue of any blurring, distortion, alteration, optical illusion, or use in composite form whether intentional or otherwise, that may occur or be produced in the taking of said picture or in any subsequent processing thereof, as well as any publication thereof, including without limitation any claims for libel or invasion of privacy.

e)   I hereby affirm that I am over the age of majority and have the right to contract in my own name. I have read the above authorization, release and agreement, prior to its execution; I fully understand the contents thereof. This agreement shall be binding upon me and my heirs, legal representatives and assigns.

Dated: _____

Signed:_____Address:_____City:_____
State: _____ Zip:_____ Phone: _____

SAMPLE LOCATION RELEASE

Having full authority to do so, I hereby grant _____ permission to use the property at _____ for the purposes of photographing and recording scenes for the production _____ during the hours of _____ on the following days:_____.

Permission includes, but is not limited to, the right to bring cast, crew, equipment, props and temporary sets onto the premises for the time specified.

Total compensation for the specified time will be: _____. If the property is available beyond the specified period, compensation will be at the rate of _____ per _____.

I understand that all items brought onto the premises will be removed at the end of the production period and that the location, including buildings, landscaping and all things associated with same will be fully returned to their original condition, except as mutually agreed upon and indicated below.

_____

_____

It is further understood that any damage to the property will become the responsibility of the production agency and any needed repair or restoration will be carried out within 14 days of the last specified day of production.

Date _____

Production Agent

Signature _____ Printed name _____ Title

_____Address _____ Phone number

_____

Property Agent

Signature _____ Printed name_____ Title

_____

Address _____ Phone number

SAMPLE INJURY RELEASE

I, _____ have voluntarily applied to participate in the above activity. I acknowledge that the nature of the activity may expose me to hazards or risks that may result in my illness; personal injury or death and I understand and appreciate the nature of such hazards and risks.

In consideration of my participation in the above activity, with the exception of gross negligence, I hereby accept all risk to my health and of my injury or death that may result from such participation and I hereby release "Big J. Productions," its governing board, officers, employees and their representatives from any and all liability to me, my personal representatives, estate, heirs, next of kin, and assigns for any and all claims and causes of action for loss of or damage to my property and for any and all illness or injury to my person, including my death, that may result from or occur during my participation in this or any activity of Big J. Productions, its governing board, officers, employees, or representatives, or otherwise.

I further agree to follow all safety instructions and procedures and indemnify and hold harmless " Big J. Productions" and its governing board, officers, employees, and representatives from liability for the injury or death of any person(s) and damage to property that may result from my negligent or intentional act or omission while participating in the described activity. I also understand that I may refuse to participate in any activity I deem excessively "dangerous" (meaning any activity above and beyond basic theatrical fighting that can be easily seen as to cause me physical harm).

 I HAVE CAREFULLY READ THIS AGREEMENT AND UNDERSTAND IT TO BE A RELEASE OF ALL CLAIMS AND CAUSES OF ACTION FOR MY INJURY OR DEATH OR DAMAGE TO MY PROPERTY THAT OCCURS WHILE PARTICIPATING IN THE DESCRIBED ACTIVITY AND IT OBLIGATES ME TO INDEMNIFY THE PARTIES NAMED FOR ANY LIABILITY FOR INJURY OR DEATH OF ANY PERSON AND DAMAGE TO PROPERTY CAUSED BY MY NEGLIGENT OR INTENTIONAL ACT OR OMISSION.

Signature of Participant:

_____

Date signed: _____

Signature of Parent/Guardian *Minors must have Parent/Guardian signature:

_____

Sample Notices of Film Shoot:

NOTICE OF FILM SHOOT

On 01/11/09 TimeCode Mechanics will be shooting a our film **Back Kick**. This film will include scenes of martial arts, stunts and action. This is to let you know what will be happening this day. We will be shooting on the corner of Clark and Lake from 11:30 am to 5:00pm.

This project will not interfere with the day to day workings of your businesses or home, but we wanted to inform you as to what would be happening on this day so that if you were to run across our production you will know what is happening.

Thank you for your time. For more information please visit us on the web at www.timecodemechanics.com. If you would like to help out please let us know as we still need extras for various scenes.

NOTICE: FILMING IN PROGRESS

Please note that TimeCode Mechanics is in the progress of shooting the independent action, horror, comedy **"Back Kick"** in this location. By entering this location, you hereby give your consent to be videotaped, photographed and/or recorded.

You grant the producer and their assignees and all in association with the production the unrestricted right of use of the images and recordings of your image, likeness and/or voice, to create, exhibit and distribute by any means they chose without compensation.

You hereby release the producer, their assignees and all in association with the production of any and all claims or causes of legal action without limitations including libel, defamation, invasion of privacy or right of publicity."

About the Author

Nathyn Brendan Masters is graduate of Columbia College Chicago's film and video program. Masters has shot several feature films including a martial arts action movie called *"Wages of Sin"* in 2006, an action horror film called, "Epitaph Bread and Salt" based on the comic book series of the same name and an action thriller called "Crisis Function". Masters vlogs and produces films on his Youtube channels "TimeCode Mechanics" and his namesake channel "Nathyn Brendan Masters,". Masters currently writes and draws comic books and role playing games for Night Phoenix Press.

Action Filmmaking Presents:

The Youtube Producer's Handbook

2nd Edition

By Nathyn Brendan Masters

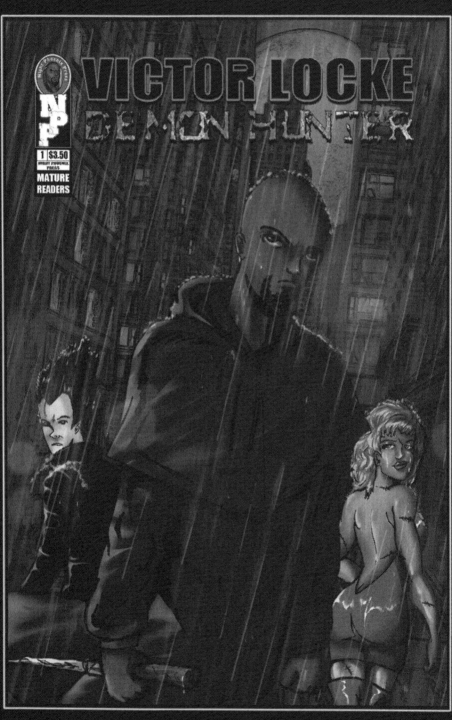

Action Filmmaking Presents:

The Youtube Producer's Handbook

Handbook

2nd Edition

Printed in Great Britain
by Amazon